How to Work with Your Court:

A Guide for Child Welfare Agency Administrators

2nd Edition

By Mark Hardin, J.D.
With Diane Boyd Rauber, M.Ed., J.D.

ABA Center on Children and the Law

National Child Welfare Resource Center on Legal and Judicial Issues...
a program of the Children's Bureau

ABA Center on Children and the Law
740 15th Street, NW
Washington, D.C. 20005-1022
(202) 662-1720 phone
(202) 662-1755 fax

The ABA Center on Children and the Law, a program of the ABA Young Lawyers Division, was established in 1978. Its mission is to improve the quality of life of children through advancements in law, justice, and public policy.

Copyright © 2004 by the American Bar Association

ISBN 1-59031-448-4

This publication was made possible by a grant from Administration for Children, Youth, and Families of the United States Department of Health and Human Services. The views expressed herein should not be construed as representing the policy of the United States Government or of the American Bar Association.

Design by the Center for Clear Communication, Inc., Rockville, Maryland

Contents

Acknowledgements 3
    Acknowledgements for the Second Edition 3
    Acknowledgements for the First Edition 4

Introduction 7

Working with Your Court: Making It a Priority 9

General Strategies for Working with Courts 13
    Meetings with the Judge 13
    Working with Other Key Court Staff 18
    Developing Special Projects with the Court 19
    Strategies for Educating Judges and Agency Attorneys 23
    Training Workers to Perform Better in Court 31
    Sharing Information with the Court 32
    Cooperation with Juvenile Courts Regarding Legislation 33
    Working to Systematically Improve Juvenile Courts 35
    Using Your Attorneys to Help You Work with Courts 36
    Use of Paralegals or Other Specialized Staff 38
    Appeals 40

Important Issues for Court and Agency Collaboration 49
    Improving Compliance with Federal Child Welfare Law 49
    Caseworker Waiting Time 74
    Convenience of Expert Witnesses — Witness Waiting Time 79
    Making Sure That Experts Are Well Prepared to Testify 81
    Access to Court 81
    Getting Judges to Accept Child Witness Reforms 84

Contents

    Limiting Excess Judicial Interference with Casework and
    Resource Allocation 86
    Improving the Agency's Success Rate in Court 89
    Special Projects to Alleviate Delays in Achieving the Termination
    of Parental Rights 91
    Agency-Court Collaboration in CFSRs and PIPs 94

Understanding the Juvenile Courts 97

    What Judges Want from Agencies 97
    Judges' Pet Peeves and What You Can Do About Them 100
    What You Can Do to Make Your Judges' Jobs Easier 109
    What Is the *Proper* Relationship Between the Agency and the Court? .. 118
    What Is the Legitimate Oversight Role of the Court? 121
    Juvenile Court Reform Efforts 122

Improving Agency Legal Representation 133

    Demanding Better Services from Attorneys and Making the Issue
    an Agency Priority 135
    Specific Services That Attorneys Should Provide in Child
    Welfare Cases 135
    Things for Administrators to Do to Get the Type of Legal
    Representation That Agencies Need 138
    Systemic Issues in Legal Representation for Child Welfare Agencies 144

Conclusion 147

About the Authors 149

Appendix: Where to Go for Additional Advice and
Information 151

    Judicial and Bar Organizations 151
    Federal Contacts 152

Bibliography 157

Index 159

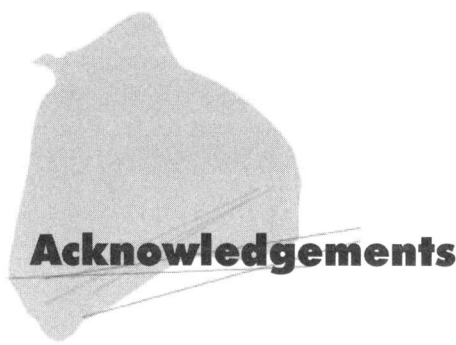

Acknowledgements

Acknowledgements for the Second Edition

This book was prepared through the National Child Welfare Resource Center on Legal and Judicial Issues, a federally funded project of the ABA Center on Children and the Law. The Resource Center has been made possible by a grant from the Administration for Children and Families of the United States Department of Health and Human Services.

Diane Boyd Rauber prepared most of the revisions and additions for the second edition. Members of the professional staff at the ABA Center on Children and the Law also provided invaluable suggestions and assistance. Mimi Laver provided guidance and support as we planned this updated edition.

Further, a number of our comments about improving the legal representation of agencies were based on Mimi's book, *Foundations for Success: Strengthening Your Agency Attorney Office*. Althea Izawa-Hayden assisted with updating the citations, bibliography, and contact information listed in the back of the book.

Carolyn Boccella Bagin, Center for Clear Communication, Inc., designed the book. Sally Small Inada provided her usual expert oversight of the production of the book.

We also owe special thanks to Emily Cooke, our federal project officer for the National Child Welfare Resource Center on Legal and Judicial Issues, both for her commitment to improving the field of child welfare and for her support and encouragement for this second edition of the book.

Mark Hardin and Diane Boyd Rauber
September 2004

Acknowledgements for the First Edition

This book was prepared through the National Legal Resource Center for Child Welfare Programs, a federally funded project of the ABA Center on Children and the Law. The Resource Center is made possible by a grant from the Administration for Children and Families of the United States Department of Health and Human Services.

A number of federal officials and professional staff have provided invaluable help and guidance for the project. Cecilia Sudia, the project officer for the Resource Center, identified the need for the book, provided guidance during its preparation, and offered valuable comments and suggestions. Mike Ambrose, the Associate Commissioner of the Children's Bureau, supported the concept and helped to move the project forward to completion.

David Lloyd, the Director of the federal government's National Center for Child Abuse and Neglect, took the time to meticulously read a prior draft and offered numerous suggestions and corrections that have been incorporated into the book. Sandra Wilkie, an intern at the Children's Bureau, also read the draft and made many helpful comments.

Some of the ideas in this book are based on what the author has learned from conversations with hundreds of child welfare administrators, court liaison staff, judges, court administrators, and attorneys over the years. Many ideas came from interviews that the author conducted specifically for the purpose of preparing this book.

Jack Ahearn, Jan Floury, David Gordon, Linda K. Harris, Renie Herman, Sandra Hodge, Rodney M. Johnson, Mary Ann Nee, Anita St. Onge, Donald

Acknowledgements

Schmidt, Jane Thompson, Katherine Tucker, and Patricia Wright all were interviewed at length and provided information that appears in this book.

A number of people not only were interviewed, but also reviewed a prior draft of the book. Those persons, listed in alphabetical order, were:

- ❖ Honorable Michael Anderegg, Marquette County Probate Court, Marquette, Michigan

- ❖ Ron Apol, Kent County Juvenile Court, Grand Rapids, Michigan

- ❖ Honorable Arthur M. Birken, Seventeenth Judicial Circuit of Florida, Fort Lauderdale, Florida

- ❖ Donald N. Duquette, Esq., Child Advocacy Law Clinic, University of Michigan Law School, Ann Arbor, Michigan

- ❖ Bonnie Hommrich, Department of Social Services, Louisville, Kentucky

- ❖ Rodney M. Johnson, Esq., Department of Health and Rehabilitative Services, Pensacola, Florida

- ❖ Maryjane Link, Pittsford, New York

- ❖ Judith Maynard, Division of Family Services, Salt Lake City, Utah

- ❖ MaryAnn Robison, Dauphin County Social Services for Children and Youth, Harrisburg, Pennsylvania

- ❖ Honorable Gerald E. Rouse, Colfax County Court, Schuyler, Nebraska

- ❖ Patricia L. Rideout and Linda Markowiac, Esq., Lucas County Children's Services, Maumee, Ohio

- ❖ Peggy Sanford, Esq., Department of Health and Rehabilitative Services, Marianne, Florida

Acknowledgements

- ❖ Linda Sunday, Children's Services Division, Salem, Oregon

- ❖ Honorable Paul R. Wohlford, Juvenile Court, Bristol, Tennessee

The reviewers' comments, reflecting a wealth of insights and practical experience, provided many helpful additions and corrected many errors in the prior draft.

Two of the above reviewers also suggested there be a book simultaneously directed to agencies, courts, and advocates, on how to work together. Two more suggested the need for a parallel book directed to judges, on how to work with agencies. These are good suggestions, especially the latter one, and perhaps we will secure funding to develop such books in the future.

The professional staff at the ABA Center on Children and the Law also reviewed prior drafts and offered invaluable suggestions. Jane Feller, June Mickens, Robert Horowitz, Marianne Takas, Sarah Kaplan, Sally Inada, Debra Ratterman, and Howard Davidson all provided essential ideas and corrections.

Nancy Bernard, formerly with the Center, provided professional proofreading and copyediting. Special thanks are due to Sally Inada for her expert oversight of the production of the book and to Kendra John-Baptiste for her highly skilled and meticulous efforts in preparing it for publication.

Of course, the opinions expressed in this book are those of the author and do not necessarily reflect the views of the reviewers, the federal government, or the American Bar Association.

Mark Hardin

Introduction

This book presents a challenge for child welfare administrators. It has been written for those with special dedication and courage. That is, it is for administrators who are not overly intimidated by lawyers and judges, and who are willing to work hard to improve agency-court relationships.

Most of all, it is for those who put the welfare of maltreated children above all other considerations.

Working with Your Court: Making It a Priority

> Some of my staff said that problems with the courts couldn't be fixed. But we have solved many. Others said those problems weren't our concern. But abused and neglected children are our concern — and problems with our courts were hurting those children.

In recent years, the legal system has become increasingly involved in child welfare cases. Today, courts are required to hold more hearings, decide more issues, and deal with more advocates than ever before. As a result, the work of child welfare agencies and juvenile courts has become intertwined.

In the early and mid-1970's, a typical child welfare case required only one court hearing. Placement of endangered children into foster care was considered a goal in itself, and the only hearing thought to be needed was the hearing where the court authorized out-of-home placement. Because agencies' legal goals could be satisfied by a single, usually uncontested, hearing, relatively little direct involvement with the courts was required.

Since the late 1970's, the emphasis on finding permanent homes for children in foster care has transformed the role of the courts in child welfare cases. This trend was accelerated by the enactment of the Adoption Assistance and Child Welfare Act of 1980, Public Law 96-272 and further refined by the implementation of the Adoption and Safe Families Act (ASFA), Public Law 103-89 in 1997. Today, to prevent needless removal of children from their homes, courts must review whether agencies have made "reasonable efforts" to prevent placement. To ensure that children are not left adrift in foster care, courts must periodically review cases involving children in their care. To legally free a child for adoption when it is clear that a child cannot be safely returned home, courts must conduct a rigorous, time consuming, and often contested termination of parental rights hearing. Because of the stringent timelines set forth in ASFA, every interaction between the agency and court is important.

Of course, this growing involvement of courts has a major impact on agency practice and administration in child welfare cases. As courts become more involved in making decisions, the quality of agencies' advocacy becomes increasingly critical to successful outcomes for families and children. As court proceedings become more complex, agencies face added burdens in time and expense.

Whether or not you are comfortable with the changing role of the courts, you need to think carefully about how to cope with the new situation. Among other things, you need to concentrate on how to help caseworkers achieve better results in court, ensure that court proceedings do not needlessly consume caseworkers' time, and assist courts in fulfilling the requirements of federal law.

Consider the following situations:

> **Example 1:** In agency X, caseworkers who come to court for periodic review hearings routinely spend their entire morning or afternoon waiting for the judge to get to their case. When the case finally comes up, the caseworker and agency attorney usually spend about five minutes explaining the case to the judge. After the worker has waited for an entire morning or afternoon for the review to begin, the judge often simply continues the case to a later time. When a decision is made, the judge nearly always approves the agency's recommendations.

> **Example 2:** In agency Y, a caseworker recently presented a proposed case plan to a judge. The judge modified the plan and instructed the caseworker to enroll parents of a hyperactive child in a specific parenting program. The worker knows that the parenting program selected by the judge is inappropriate because it is geared toward more normal children. Yet the worker feels unable to explain this problem to the judge.

Example 3: In agency Z, a caseworker is convinced that a child can never safely go home and thinks he should be placed for adoption. The caseworker believes that, under ASFA, it is reasonable in this case to make no effort to reunify the family. However, the worker believes the judge will require the agency to attempt reunification and does not seek a judicial finding that no efforts are reasonable in this case.

Each of the above examples describes problems that are debilitating to the agency. These problems needlessly consume valuable agency resources and are harmful to children.

This book discusses what child welfare administrators can do about such problems. The basic thesis of the book is as follows:

> Child welfare agencies' working relationships with courts are vital to agencies' ability to successfully protect children;
>
> There is much that child welfare administrators can do to improve working relationships with courts; but
>
> To achieve real progress with the courts, administrators must make working with the courts a top priority.

In other words, administrators must not passively or cynically accept problems with courts. Administrators need to ask the following questions:

❖ Are at least some of our problems with the legal system avoidable?

❖ What can we do to improve the situation?

❖ Will the likely results be worth our time and trouble?

This book is designed to help administrators answer such questions. It offers specific suggestions for working with the legal system.

General Strategies for Working with Courts

Over the years, we've learned that there are very definite right and wrong ways to approach the courts. I wish I'd known years ago what I know today.

There are several basic strategies for agency administrators to use in working with courts. They should be considered regardless of the specific issue or problem.

Meetings with the Judge

Perhaps the most obvious problem-solving strategy is to meet with judges and court administrators to search for solutions. This strategy is an important one, but doing it successfully is not as simple as it sounds. Communications with courts can be tricky, and there are right and wrong ways to approach judges. The following are some tips to keep in mind when initiating and participating in such meetings.

Be specific and task oriented. Judges are generally very concrete in their approach to problem solving. Meetings should be short and to the point. Avoid a general "gripe session." If there is a problem, be prepared to describe it precisely. If the judge questions the existence or seriousness of the problem, be prepared to offer specific examples to illustrate the problem.

Present a written agenda. With many judges, it helps to present a written agenda for meetings, setting forth issues to be discussed. A clear and thoughtful agenda can help convince the judge of the importance of the meeting and can persuade the judge to attend in person rather than to send a subordinate. Receiving an agenda in advance, the judge will have the opportunity to think about the issue(s) and obtain information and advice from subordinates before coming to the meeting.

Here is an example of how a problem might be documented and described:

> We have calculated that our foster care caseworkers wait for review hearings for an average of three hours each time they come to court. The hearings themselves are often less than a half hour. Sometimes, after the workers wait, the hearings are simply rescheduled.
>
> We estimate that caseworkers are spending approximately 10% of their time in court, which makes it harder for them to work with clients and actually carry out their case plans.
>
> We recognize the pressure on your court calendar and that solutions to this problem are not easy. We'd like to explore ideas for alleviating this situation.

Develop concrete proposals. Beyond identifying issues for discussion, try to develop concrete proposals to address the items on the agenda. Most judges will appreciate concreteness, so long as the agency is willing to be flexible.

The following is an example of a proposal to a court:

> An agency is located far from the court and feels that it is unnecessary for its social workers and clerks to personally deliver papers to the court. After conferring with the agency attorney, an administrator proposes the following:
>
> After we remove a child from home in an emergency, we would like your permission to send in our first court report by fax. If when we remove a child in an emergency and find out that any party has an attorney, we

> would fax a copy of the report to the attorney at the same time we fax the report to the court.
>
> We also request permission occasionally to fax to the court predisposition and review hearing reports in situations where we have missed the deadline for mailing them.

There may be flaws or technical legal problems in such a proposal. But putting a specific proposal forward adds to the efficiency of the discussion.

The following is an agency's request to get a speaker onto the agenda of a judicial conference:

> Dr. William R. Flemmish is available to speak at the next statewide judicial conference and we would like to give the judges the opportunity to hear him. Dr. Flemmish is a noted expert on the adoption of "special needs" children with emotional and physical handicaps. He can explain the process for placing special needs children in adoptive homes and can also discuss the prospects for successful adoption after placement. Do you think this would be of interest to the juvenile court judges?

Concentrate on what you can do to help the court. Focus on what you can do to assist the court, not only on what the court can do for you. If you are just beginning to initiate regular meetings with the court, start out by focusing on a problem of concern to the judge rather than one of concern to the agency. For example, if you have heard the judge is unhappy with the quality of court reports and agency recommendations, a good topic for an early meeting might be how you can improve the reports and recommendations to meet the needs of the court.

Assuming that the judge makes reasonable suggestions, try to respond quickly and fully. After you have attempted to comply with the judge's requests, check back with the judge to see whether the response was satisfactory. This courtesy will motivate the judge to continue meeting and cooperating with you.

When you are offering your own proposals, be prepared to explain how they can help the court. For example, suppose that, as discussed above, you would like permission to fax certain court reports rather than delivering them to the court in person or by mail. You can offer the following explanation in support of your proposal:

> If you allow us to fax our court reports, we will be able to improve our record of getting them to you on time. We know you expect to receive those reports two days in advance of the hearing, and the use of faxes will assist our ongoing effort to comply with this requirement. Of course, we will fax or deliver the reports to the other parties at the same time that we fax them to the court.

In many places throughout the United States, agency administrators and courts have established regularly scheduled meetings. Some of these meetings are an outgrowth of various legislative mandates and grants; others have occurred because of judges' receptiveness to such meetings and the agencies' ability to keep the meetings interesting and useful to judges. Regardless of their origin, these meetings can prove fruitful for both the agency and the court.

In Nebraska, for example, the Court-Agency Collaboration Project was initiated with federal Court Improvement Project and Adoption Opportunities Grant funds. In the three counties with the highest concentration of cases, various stakeholders meet on a monthly basis to discuss system barriers and strategies for improvement. As a result of these meetings, one county has piloted in-depth preliminary protective custody hearings in all three of its courts. All three judges conduct these hearings on the same morning of the week and emphasis is placed on front loading the process.

Consult with your attorneys before submitting proposals. Talk to your attorneys in advance before submitting any written proposals to the judge. There may be technical errors in what you are proposing that need to be corrected before being sent out, especially if you are proposing changes in the court calendar, judicial procedures, or court forms. In the above example concerning permission to fax reports to the court, there may be a legal reason why the proposal is not possible, depending on your state's laws and the local court rules. Therefore, such proposals need to be discussed with the agency's attorney before being presented to the judge. On the other hand, if your attorneys are not helpful or knowledgeable, you may need to focus on improving your legal representation. This topic is discussed in a later chapter.

Make sure the right agency staff members are present when you meet with the judge. People with exact knowledge of the issues you wish to discuss should be at the meeting. In addition, if an issue of agency policy or procedure is to be discussed, administrators with power concerning the policy in question should be present. Otherwise, the judge is likely to feel the meeting has been a waste of time.

In most cases, your attorney needs to be present during meetings with the judge. For example, if you wish to discuss revisions in legal forms or changes in the court calendar, the attorney should be there to help iron out technical details.

Schedule occasional special meetings between judges and line workers. If the judge is amenable, occasionally set up special meetings between line workers and judges. The value of such meetings is that they give both judges and agency administrators a very concrete picture of the impact of the legal process on workers and their clients. Also, the workers will appreciate the opportunity to explain their concerns about the practical effect of the legal process on their work.

In addition to routine meetings between agency administrators and the judge, consider inviting your judges to serve on state or local interagency task forces. Judges can play a useful role in interdisciplinary committees addressing such issues as child fatalities, child sexual abuse, children with HIV, and interagency resource allocation. Judges can clarify legal issues, learn more about the children whose lives they affect, become more familiar with agencies and, in many cases, help bring about needed changes in county or state policy.

When judges are helpful, express your thanks. Like child welfare agency administrators and staff, judges are often criticized and seldom praised for their work. Thank you letters to judges who have gone out of their way to be helpful can be a good way to reinforce cooperation and cement good relations. Most judges will find such a letter a pleasant surprise and will remember who wrote it.

For example, one agency administrator was impressed by a judge who had taken special pains to enter detailed findings of fact in a termination of parental rights case. After the case was all over, the administrator wrote a letter explaining how unusually good the findings had been, how helpful the attorneys said the findings had been to winning the appeal, and how well the child was doing in her new adoptive home.

If the judge makes a change (e.g., in scheduling or docketing) that is helpful for your staff, consider writing the judge and explaining how pleased your staff was with the change and how much you appreciated it.

Working with Other Key Court Staff

While it is critical to meet with judges on important problems, judges cannot be expected to attend very frequent and extensive meetings with agency staff. If frequent meetings are needed to work out issues in great detail, most judges will delegate court staff to attend and report back. In addition, many judges prefer to attend meetings only if top-level agency staff members are present. Thus, much of the work with the court is likely to be conducted with court staff assigned by the judge. Except for meetings with top-level agency staff for the purpose of dealing with major issues, do not expect the judge to attend.

There are wide variations in the staffing of juvenile courts and therefore it is difficult to generalize about who the judge might assign to work with the agency. Possibilities can include court administrators, administrative staff, lawyers employed by the court for research or special projects, social workers employed by the courts, or Court Appointed Special Advocate (CASA) coordinators.

When meeting with court staff, begin by exchanging information about your respective job duties and responsibilities. The designated court employee may be serving as no more than a conduit for the exchange of information with the judge. On the other hand, the employee may have considerable authority to propose or make changes within the court. The employee may have a strong grasp of technical matters being discussed and may be an excellent substitute for the judge.

Developing Special Projects with the Court

In many cases, it is not enough to meet with the court in order to solve problems. Some problems emerge that cannot be solved through discussion alone. Rather, more intensive joint efforts are required.

To respond to particularly complex issues or intractable problems, many agencies and courts have developed intensive joint projects. That is, agencies and courts have assigned staff to work together to try to solve specific problems. Often, such special projects are created during agency-court meetings. Agency and court staff assigned to special projects typically report their progress during agency-court meetings attended by judges and high level administrators.

Many projects have been developed as a result of the agency-court collaboration achieved through federal Court Improvement Project grants, which are designed to improve state courts' handling of child abuse and neglect cases. In addition, the requirements of the Child and Family Services Reviews, conducted by the Children's Bureau to determine states' conformity with federal child welfare requirements, have also enhanced agency-court collaboration and resulted in special projects.

Consider the following example:

> In County A, the agency and the court are, for different reasons, both dissatisfied concerning agency reports to the court. The court is dissatisfied with the substance of many reports and the fact they are filed too late. The agency feels the court does not pay sufficient attention to the reports it files. To deal with these problems, agency and court staff members are directed to work together to achieve the following goals:
>
> ❖ to improve the form for court reports,
>
> ❖ to develop sample forms that have been skillfully completed, and

❖ to agree on protocol concerning when and how the reports must be submitted.

The agency believes that by providing reports more satisfactory to the court, judges will rely more on the reports when making decisions.

A related purpose of joint agency-court projects can be problem clarification. Sometimes when courts and agencies experience difficulties working together, the exact cause of the difficulties are not clear. The problem may lie with the agency or the court, or both. Agency and court staff may need to work together to figure out exactly why problems exist.

Here is an example of a special project to clarify and resolve a problem:

In County B, both the agency and the court are dissatisfied about the delivery of homemaker services to families. The agency feels that the court sometimes expects homemaker services in inappropriate situations and, more generally, the court is highly inconsistent in requesting the use of homemakers. The court feels the agency too often disregards judicial recommendations and the agency itself is inconsistent and irrational in deciding when to use homemakers.

Both court and agency staff members are assigned to try to help clarify the situation. Court staff members are assigned to examine selected closed court files and to talk to judges, in order to determine under what circumstances the court typically requests or orders homemaker services.

Agency staff members are assigned to examine the delivery of homemaker services in order to determine how its decisions are made, what priorities for services exist, and the extent of delays and waiting lists. After this information is assembled, judges and key agency administrative staff will meet to discuss ways to improve the situation.

Agencies must understand that in the process of working with the courts to solve mutual problems, they cannot discuss specific pending cases with court personnel. Such discussions are called *ex parte communications* and they violate both attorney and judicial ethics. An *ex parte communication* occurs when one side discusses a case with the judge without the opposing party present. Except in certain emergency situations, such discussions are improper.

Agency personnel and court staff are free to discuss general problems and issues without reference to specific cases. They may discuss closed cases as illustrative examples of current problems, or statistical summaries of agency or court performance. They also may discuss purely logistical concerns about specific cases, such as the timely transmission of forms or files. However, there should be no discussion of the facts of an open case, particularly when information may be shared with the judge.

Apart from judicial ethics, some judges are reluctant to work on special projects with the agency, because that might make it look like the court is favoring the agency. Perhaps the best way to dispel that concern is to invite others to participate, such as key attorneys for parents, guardians ad litem, and representatives of interested private organizations.

Another type of joint project may involve cooperation in gathering and exchanging statistics. For example, both the agency and the court may want to be made aware of cases involving children who have been in foster care for more than 12 months and who have not been freed for adoption. Either the court or the agency, or both, may have information systems that gather such information. Perhaps the court's information system includes data useful to the agency and vice versa.

There are examples of successful agency-court cooperation in gathering and exchanging data:

> Utah is upgrading its centralized data collection system to allow for cross communication and data sharing between the court and the child welfare agency. Called CARE, for "Court Agency Records Exchange," this Internet-based system consists of various modules, which can capture different types of data.
>
> Similarly, the Georgia Child Placement Project sponsored a case plan pilot project, the State of Georgia Case Plan Reporting System (CPRS), which allows caseworkers and judges to access individual case plans through a password system. This system allows the parties to leave the courtroom with a completed case plan. The system has been

implemented statewide, with more than 16,000 case plans residing in the system.

Still other types of joint projects enhance or pool resources:

> The Maine District Court is collaborating with the child welfare agency on the Child Abuse and Neglect Evaluators Project (CANEP) to improve the quality and timeliness of court-ordered parental capacity evaluators in child protection cases. All participating evaluators utilize a research-based evaluation protocol developed by the court's clinical consultant.

> An example of resource pooling is Hawaii's Project Visitation. The Family Court and child welfare agency have teamed with legal services to develop this project, which facilitates contacts and strengthens the bonds between siblings placed in different foster homes.

These types of projects require real initiative and creativity, as well as flexibility on the part of the administrators supporting it.

A common pitfall in the development of joint projects is that after some initial momentum, the efforts fall apart. For example:

> In one urban midwest county, the agency and court formed a joint permanency planning committee. At first, this was a highly successful project that resulted in a good manual and a commitment to work together on issues as they came up.

> However, after about four years, the committee fell apart due to a lack of leadership; there was no consistent effort by someone to see that the committee met and followed up on agreements. The manual is now useless because it was not kept up to date.

When a joint cooperation project is begun, a person from each side needs to be continually assigned the job of keeping it active. If a project is no longer necessary, it is better consciously to disband it than to allow it to fall into disuse.

Strategies for Educating Judges and Agency Attorneys

Another way for agencies to achieve better results in court and improve their relationships with judges is by helping to educate judges. Agencies also need to educate their attorneys, so the attorneys can more effectively represent the agency.

Joint Training

Agencies should be aware of how difficult it is to conduct successful training programs involving agency staff, judges, and lawyers. Very often, when agencies attempt to conduct "joint training," only a sprinkling of judges and lawyers actually participate. The audience ends up consisting almost entirely of agency employees and other social service professionals.

The most important reason why lawyers and judges are reluctant to attend joint training is that they feel that it will not provide them with information that is useful in their day-to-day work. Judges want training that helps them to manage their dockets efficiently and to reach legally correct decisions. Lawyers want to know about recent cases and legal arguments they can make in court. Joint training usually does not provide this type of information.

Further, judges typically feel most comfortable being trained by other judges and lawyers feel most comfortable being trained by other lawyers. Judges may believe that only other judges have the experience to understand what information is useful to them. Lawyers may have similar feelings.

One strategy to overcome the resistance of judges and lawyers to participate in joint training is to make the judges and lawyers "trainers." For example, one agency invited its four juvenile court judges to sit on a panel to react to a presentation by a noted speaker at a training program for child welfare workers. The agency did so not only to expose its staff to the judges' views on the subject, but also to make sure that:

❖ the judges heard the presentation by the noted speaker;

- ❖ the judges refined their own thoughts on the subject of the presentation in advance;
- ❖ the judges carefully thought about the presentation in order to respond to it; and
- ❖ the judges heard the views of agency administrators and caseworkers.

By using the judges to educate caseworkers, the agency was also educating its judges.

If judges are to be used as trainers, it is important to be very specific about the topic of the training. It is also prudent to find out about others' past experiences in using particular judges as trainers. There are a few judges who habitually disrupt training by expounding on their personal philosophy instead of addressing the training topic.

Another useful strategy for joint training is to craft the training so it truly will be of mutual interest to the court and agency. To persuade attorneys and judges to attend, consider calling it something other than training, such as a *seminar*, *colloquium*, or *dialogue*. To make the training work, limit the total length of the sessions and make sure the agenda deals only with issues of joint concern to courts and agencies. For example, the training might deal with such issues as what a good court report looks like, how to combat case delays, how caseworkers should present themselves in court, topics that a caseworker may discuss with a judge outside of court, and how the agency can help the judicial process to operate more efficiently.

To plan for organized panel discussions, work with the court to develop a good list of questions to be addressed by a panel of agency administrators, lead workers, agency attorneys, court administrators, and judges. Members of the audience, including a larger group of caseworkers and supervisors, can be requested to make comments and ask follow-up questions.

Again, get commitments from judges and lawyers to attend as major participants rather than as audience members. It also helps if prominent judges and bar leaders can be persuaded to send letters urging key attorneys and judges to attend. For example, helpful letters might be solicited from the Chief Justice of the State Supreme Court, the president of the state's juvenile judges' organization, and the president of the agency attorneys' organization.

In recent years, jurisdictions have planned joint trainings that utilize each group's strengths and result in the development of action plans. The state of Washington has utilized this approach for many years. Through the regional Reasonable Efforts Symposia, local interdisciplinary planning teams, with the assistance of the University of Washington School of Social Work, conduct collaborative meetings where judicial panels present, jurisdictions report on action plans, and the planning teams refine or develop new action plans.

Agency Involvement in Judicial and Bar Conferences and Educational Programs

Rather than concentrating on persuading judges or lawyers to come to training sessions you conduct, it may be more productive to offer to help with training routinely provided for judges and attorneys. For example, if there are regular meetings or training programs for the state organization of juvenile court judges, the agency may be able to appear and make a presentation.

If you can arrange to make a presentation at a judicial or bar conference, you need to make a special effort to tailor your presentation to a legal audience. You must present something that both will hold the audience's attention and will encourage the organization to invite you to speak in the future.

In the following example, an agency misused its opportunity to address judges. The speaker, a child welfare administrator, had been asked to describe the agency's services for families and children:

> The child welfare administrator's talk outlined the agency's theories about providing services. The administrator also explained some of the agency's long run ideas for improving services. During the presentation, the judges were polite but didn't seem very interested. The administrator ascribed this reaction to the judges' disinterest in child welfare.
>
> Actually, many of the judges would have appreciated a more concrete presentation, with practical information. The judges would have liked a description of the different types of services currently available to families and children who come before their courts. They would have liked to learn which types of problems each service was designed to address and in what parts of the state each service is available.

> If the judges had been presented with the practical realities about services, they would have received information they could have used in their day-to-day work. Knowing about services would have helped them ask the right questions during review hearings. It would have helped them evaluate agency work with families in termination of parental rights cases. It might even have encouraged them to speak to county commissioners about the need to provide additional funding.
>
> After the presentation, many of the judges felt that their time had been wasted by vague generalities, social work jargon, and information of little actual use to them as judges. They felt, however, that they had given the agency an appropriate courtesy in allowing it to speak.

As the above example illustrates, involvement in training judges requires careful thought and planning. Judges and attorneys do not respond well to training designed to improve interdisciplinary understanding in a general sense. Rather than making theoretical presentations designed to improve interdisciplinary understanding, it is usually better to provide specific and practical information and hope that improved interdisciplinary understanding will be a by-product.

For example, attorneys and judges are unlikely to be interested in or profit from a presentation on family "eco maps" used by caseworkers to identify kinship and community ties. This information does not help them do their own jobs.

One particularly effective way to provide training for judges and lawyers is to recruit another judge or lawyer to make the presentation. There are judges and lawyers with a background in or understanding of child welfare casework and practice as well as the law. Judges and lawyers, like others, often respond best to presentations by their "peers." They are convinced by persons who they feel share their experience and can relate to their problems.

Many agencies have secured a prominent place on the agendas of judicial and bar groups by helping to underwrite training costs. Often, agencies have paid the costs of bringing in out-of-state speakers. Sometimes they have even have paid for that portion of the training program devoted to child welfare concerns. By taking this approach, agencies have been able to train judges who are not juvenile court specialists and who ordinarily hear little about child welfare issues.

There are both potential advantages and disadvantages in the use of outside speakers. On the positive side, outside speakers can help attract an audience. Furthermore, outside speakers can provide new ideas for dealing with local problems. On the other hand, outside speakers' ideas may be irrelevant to local circumstances.

Special care is required to ensure outside speakers address real concerns of the local agency and courts. It is not enough to select speakers who are effective presenters. You need to make it clear exactly why you have asked them to speak and what it is you want them to get across to the audience. Consider the following plan for obtaining an out-of-state speaker:

> The agency is concerned about delays in court proceedings causing children to remain a long time in foster care. The agency arranges for two speakers at a judicial conference. One is a former judge who will speak on the subject of "judicial caseflow management" in juvenile court, or how to squeeze out needless delays and increase court efficiency. The other is a psychologist who will discuss the effect of delays on children and will include anecdotes involving children who were traumatized by prolonged and indecisive court proceedings.

It takes a great deal of time to make these arrangements and to make sure the speakers cover what you want them to cover. The following are some steps you can take to ensure that the talks will be on point and relevant to local problems:

- ❖ If you are permitted to identify topics and speakers, consult thoroughly with local judges before doing so.

- ❖ Provide enough compensation to the speakers so that you can expect thorough preparation for the talk.

- ❖ Inform speakers in writing (perhaps in their contract) concerning the steps you will expect of them in preparing for the talk.

- ❖ Carefully explain the topic of the talk, both over the telephone and in writing, and explain your specific goals in arranging for the talk.

- ❖ Provide the speakers with locally relevant information. (In the above example, give the speakers some typical illustrations of needless delay in your state or locality, and explain what usually causes them.)

- ❖ Give the speakers the names and telephone numbers of judges, agency staff, and others who can provide further information about the problems in your state or locality that are relevant to the topic.

- ❖ Check back later with the speakers to confirm their understanding of the topic and make sure all needed information was provided.

- ❖ If speakers have a standard speech on the topic, review a copy of the speech in advance in order to point out local examples of problems and issues.

- ❖ When speakers arrive, do everything possible to make them feel at ease about their presentation. Relaxed speakers establish better rapport with the audience.

With extra preparation and effort, your contribution to judicial and bar training can be far more powerful and persuasive.

In addition to making sure that the presentations are useful, the agency should think about how to attract an audience for the speaker. Besides arranging for speakers with impressive credentials and coming up with interesting topics, it is helpful to include in training announcements that "recent developments" will be covered or that the presentation will provide an "update." This message conveys a sense of urgency and reassures that new material will be covered.

Providing Reference Materials for Judges and Agency Attorneys

Because the effectiveness of attorneys and judges largely depends upon their grasp of the law, the quality of available written materials can have a great effect on their performance. Agencies can play an important role in the development of judicial and attorney reference and training materials, and some states have commissioned such materials.

As the result of the numerous changes imposed by ASFA and the availability of federal Court Improvement Project funds, many states have developed benchbooks and other relevant training materials. For example, the Michigan Judicial Institute used funds from the child welfare agency to develop an adoption benchbook.

Georgia developed cross-training notebooks for judges, case managers, and attorneys who represent the agency. A large number of these benchbooks and training materials can be reviewed or obtained through the National Child Welfare Resource Center on Legal and Judicial Issues' online *National Court Improvement Catalog*, located at www.abanet.org/child/cipcatalog/home.html.

Requiring Agency Attorneys to Attend Training

Child welfare agencies should try to ensure that their attorneys attend appropriate educational programs. Of course, the agency also needs to make sure the training in question is really useful and appropriate for attorneys. To make sure, you need to check in advance with trusted attorneys who are knowledgeable about child welfare.

Agencies that employ their own lawyers can make training attendance a condition of employment. Agencies that contract for attorney services can make sure the next contract specifies the training that the attorneys are to receive. In either case, of course, there must be money to pay for the trainers and to pay for the attorneys' time while they are attending training.

Of course, many agencies do not employ or contract with their own attorneys. For example, many agencies are represented by independently elected county prosecutors. (Different types of legal representation of child welfare agencies are discussed in chapter 5, *Improving Agency Legal Representation*.) Agencies that do not employ their own attorneys must use other strategies to ensure their attendance in training.

One tactic to consider is to approach the supervisor of the attorney(s) who represent the agency in court and ask that it be policy that the attorneys attend the training. In addition, similar strategies can be used to persuade the lawyers to attend training as can be used for judges. For example, the agency may need to work closely with organizations of county attorneys and to provide part of the funding for the training.

It is appropriate for new attorneys to attend a portion of their training together with new caseworkers. This joint training helps the attorneys understand something about casework and understand the agency better. However, the attorneys also need separate training concerning technical aspects of child welfare law. A local law school, law professor, bar association, or continuing legal education program can provide this training. National bar and advocacy organizations such as the ABA Center on Children and the Law can also provide training or technical assistance for training.

Some agencies have mandatory training curricula for their attorneys just as for their caseworkers. These curricula include introductory training, advanced trial skills training, and periodic updates on child welfare law and practice. If practical, this approach is best. Informal and ongoing training efforts are also useful and important. Some ideas for training can be found in M. Laver, *Foundations for Success: Strengthening Your Agency Attorney Office* (ABA 1999). Chapter 9 of this book details the various training activities of the Santa Clara County Counsel Office Child Dependency Unit and offers various models for establishing regular meetings and providing training.

Many agencies pay for their attorneys to attend conferences put on by such organizations as the ABA Center on Children and the Law, the American Association of Public Welfare Attorneys, the National Council of Juvenile and Family Court Judges, or the National Association of Counsel for Children. This training is helpful, but not a substitute for a planned, state-specific curriculum. Unfortunately, many agencies pay for attorney training on a disorganized and inconsistent basis.

Federal Reimbursement for Training Judges or Attorneys

Sometimes an agency's expenses for educating judges or lawyers will be partially reimbursable with federal matching funds under Title IV-E of the Social Security Act. See 42 U.S.C. § 674(a)(3). For example, if an agency's training for judges involves compliance with federal foster care requirements, the agency's training expenses should be matchable as agency administrative costs. Since judges are not employees of the agency, the agency is not eligible for the relatively high federal match for staff training. However, the agency should qualify for matching funds for its administrative costs, because the communication with judges is a necessary expense in administering the Title IV-E Program.

If the agency is training lawyers who are employees of the agency, the agency can draw the higher federal match for staff training. But if the attorneys are not agency employees, then matching funds are available as ordinary administrative costs, as with training of judges.

Training Workers to Perform Better in Court

Another essential way to obtain better results in court is to train caseworkers to improve their court performance. Obviously, agencies are more successful in court when workers do a good job at preparing cases and testifying. In addition, when workers are well prepared, judges are more pleasant and tension is alleviated.

While nearly every state agency provides some legal training for caseworkers, some agencies do it far better than others. The following are some desirable features of legal training for caseworkers:

- ❖ A curriculum should be jointly designed by attorneys knowledgeable about child welfare and non-lawyer experts who specialize in child welfare training. The curriculum should include a variety of techniques, including lectures, role plays, games, and exercises.

- ❖ The introductory portion of the curriculum (requiring at least two days to present) should be mandatory for beginning caseworkers, and refresher presentations should be mandatory for all caseworkers on an annual or biannual basis.

- ❖ Workers should be tested for their mastery of the curriculum and be expected to pass the test. Successful completion should be a condition of employment.

❖ A special state-specific legal reference handbook should be prepared for and distributed to caseworkers. The handbook should provide a readable description of the court process and of key legal rules that apply in child abuse cases. For example, both Iowa and New York have developed legal reference books for caseworkers with agency funds.

A helpful non-state-specific monograph on the courts designed for caseworkers is J. Feller, et al., *Working With the Courts in Child Protection* (U.S. Dept. of Health and Hum. Serv. 1992).

When training is being offered on a local basis, it is especially important to involve the court in both planning and actually making presentations. This strategy not only can help sensitize the judges to agency concerns, as explained above, but also can enhance the quality of the training. The court can help identify needed training topics and can clarify such things as local judicial procedures, how the judges decide cases, the judges' pet peeves, and so forth.

When planning training that is at least partially legal in its focus, consider inviting the court to be an official co-sponsor. Invite the court to propose training topics and to help plan a portion of the curriculum. Permit the court to identify and provide trainers.

Sharing Information with the Court

Another important strategy in working with courts is to share information concerning how the agency works. Some agency administrators are reluctant to share such information, feeling that providing it will encourage the court to interfere improperly with agency decisionmaking.

Indeed, in the earlier example, in which an agency administrator spoke only theoretically about services rather than actually describing them, the agency may have wished to withhold information to avoid possible judicial interference. On the other hand, some administrators feel that being open with the courts makes judges more understanding of agency problems and helps judges perform better in court.

Another important way to provide information to courts is to send out agency regulations and policy manuals. Rather than sending out entire manuals to all judges, however, state agencies should let judges know these are available upon request or periodically send judges interesting excerpts on topics they will find especially useful.

For example, consider sending judges excerpts from agency policy concerning confidentiality and adoption subsidy. If you choose to do this, accompany the excerpts with a short memo explaining why they are of interest to judges. Judges will appreciate that these materials are available even if they do not request complete copies.

Cooperation with Juvenile Courts Regarding Legislation

Sometimes it is helpful for child welfare agencies to work with judges on appropriations and legislative issues. On the local level, many judges who handle child abuse and neglect cases are socially prominent and have credibility with such local governing boards as county commissions. Sometimes, when local judges are convinced that added agency staff or services would enhance the judges' own ability to administer justice (as well as helping families and children), the judges can help the agency.

Similarly, on the state level, judges' organizations often have credibility with legislatures and governors. Sometimes judges' organizations are willing to offer testimony at legislative hearings that is useful to the agency. While judicial testimony must deal with issues of specific concern to judges, there are times that the concerns of judges and agencies converge. For example, consider the following:

> The child welfare agency of State X wants to convince the legislature it needs additional access to drug treatment services for mothers. Judges also are frustrated because the lack of services sometimes forces them to make decisions that are not best for children.
>
> After discussion with the child welfare agency, the State X Council of Juvenile and Family Court Judges decides to offer testimony to the legislature.

The Council will testify as follows:

> In child abuse and neglect cases, judges often are compelled to order children removed from home because of drug-related abuse or neglect. When this happens, judges often approve, recommend, or order drug treatment for parents. Yet, when cases come back to court for review, parents often are still on waiting lists for drug treatment.
>
> The delays in treatment compel judges to delay final decisions about children's future. During the time when parents are waiting for treatment and up to the time that treatment has been completed, judges cannot order children to be returned home and cannot legally free them for adoption. This delay makes it impossible for judges to make these decisions within the times prescribed by ASFA.
>
> In effect, the lack of drug treatment services for parents causes children needlessly to remain in foster care. This situation is hard on the courts, is bad for the children, and is ultimately expensive to the state since the state pays for the needlessly lengthy foster care.

Judicial testimony can be quite compelling and may help legislators grasp the seriousness of a problem. Furthermore, such testimony is clearly ethical in most states. See American Bar Association, *Model Code of Judicial Conduct*, Canon 4(C)(1) (1990); American Bar Association, *Model Code of Judicial Conduct*, Section 4(B) (1972). Sometimes judges feel more comfortable testifying if you have arranged for the legislative committee to make a written request for their testimony.

Similarly, administrators should consider supporting juvenile courts' requests for resources. Administrators can sometimes help by explaining how overcrowded dockets cause court delays and needlessly prolong children's stay in foster care. The agency can explain these problems both to the legislature and to top level court administrators. Consider the following example:

> The juvenile court judges in State Y are frustrated with increasingly overcrowded dockets in child welfare cases. The State Administrative Office of the Courts (AOC) has the power to ask the legislature to fund several additional judgeships but does not feel it is necessary. The judges are trying to convince the AOC to change its mind.

> The director of the state child welfare agency meets with the president of the state's Council of Juvenile and Family Court Judges and offers to write a letter to the AOC, supporting the court's request for additional judges. In the letter, the administrator would explain the practical consequences of not having the additional judges. The letter would give examples of children being needlessly kept in foster care because of court delays, and the costs of the delays to the state agency.

Of course, this kind of cooperation is easier to achieve in some states than others. Administrators need to be aware of the possibility.

Working to Systematically Improve Juvenile Courts

Agencies are hurt by inefficient courts lacking expertise in juvenile law. Inefficient courts lacking sensitivity to child welfare issues delay cases, ignore inconveniences inflicted on caseworkers, inappropriately refuse to terminate parental rights, and refuse to take steps for the protection of child witnesses.

While knowledgeable judges may be inclined to question the decisions and activities of the agency, they are also more sensitive to the needs of children and agencies.

Agencies sometimes have the opportunity to support broad juvenile court reform efforts. For example, the courts may be interested in creating a specialized family court, which will help develop more knowledgeable judges with a greater interest in working closely with agencies.

While agencies cannot take a leading or principal role on these issues, they sometimes can help stimulate and support change. Agencies can support social science studies of juvenile courts, including studies of how courts and agencies interact.

When reform initiatives are underway within the courts, agencies can offer their perspective, knowledge, data, and support. Agency-generated data on court delays or caseworker waiting time, for example, can be helpful to court reform efforts.

To be involved in court improvement efforts, agencies need to have a basic understanding of key issues regarding court reform. Later sections of this book briefly discuss key court reform issues.

Using Your Attorneys to Help You Work with Courts

Agencies can most effectively work out problems with courts when they are actively supported by knowledgeable attorneys. This section discusses what attorneys should be doing for you in resolving specific difficulties. Agency attorneys should:

❖ help identify the exact source of agency difficulties with the courts;

❖ develop suggestions to solve the problems; and

❖ join the agency in communicating with the court.

Many of the problems between agencies and courts involve, at least in part, technical legal issues that agency staff may not fully appreciate. Agency attorneys can help identify and explain such barriers and also can try to work out solutions.

Consider the following example:

> In State Z, the state has failed a federal review because many court orders authorizing the removal of children from their homes do not include findings that the agency has made "reasonable efforts" to prevent placement.
>
> State Z's child welfare agency has asked the courts to use court order forms that include printed language reciting that the agency has made reasonable efforts. The judges do not want such language to be preprinted into their forms, and the agency does not understand why.

In the above situation, the agency needs its lawyer to be present during discussions with judges. A good agency attorney should be able to narrow the problem and explain to the agency exactly why judges do not want to use the preprinted form.

In this case, the attorney might be able to explain to the agency that:

> The judges are concerned that the preprinted form calls upon them to automatically make findings when the findings may not be based on evidence presented to the court. It is improper for judges to make findings unsupported by actual evidence.

Besides helping to uncover and clarify the judges' concerns to the agency, the agency lawyer should be expected to help propose legally sound solutions. In the above case, the agency attorney might suggest the following:

> The agency will develop a proposed form that has blanks for the judges to determine whether <u>or not</u> the agency has made reasonable efforts and, as required by State X law, to specify what those efforts were. To make it easy for the judges to fill in the blanks, the agency's court report will provide the precise information needed by the judges to fill in the blanks.
>
> In other words, the agency's reports will include the information the judge needs to describe what the agency's reasonable efforts were. Agency caseworkers, with the help of the agency attorneys, will provide testimony backing up all of the information in the report.
>
> When the judge finds the agency's efforts to have been sufficient and written information to be accurate, the judge can simply cross-reference to the agency report in the court order authorizing removal. For example, when the parties stipulate (agree) to the accuracy of the report, the court order can simply state that "reasonable efforts were made to prevent removal and to reunify the family as described in the agency report dated...." This will satisfy both due process and federal law.

If the parties do not agree to the accuracy of the report but the agency provides convincing evidence to support it, the court order can still cross reference to the report, using the identical language quoted above. In either case, the court order will meet federal audit requirements and will conform to proper judicial procedure.

After the agency has decided upon a strategy to address a problem, it should seek the help of its attorney in refining and implementing the strategy. In the above example, if the agency wants to try to get the courts to strengthen their orders, the attorney might do the following:

- Draft a revised form court order.

- Circulate the draft within the agency and make needed changes.

- Submit the proposed court order to the appropriate judicial committee and to influential judges to persuade them to approve it.

- Talk to the key judges and appear in person at meetings of relevant committees, explaining the reasons for the proposed change.

- Make further revisions if requested to do so.

During the entire process, the attorney would be communicating frequently with its agency administration. Such collaboration empowers the agency by helping it understand the concerns of the court, giving it a means to express its own concerns, and helping it find solutions.

No doubt, some agency administrators would be delighted to have such help from their attorneys as described above, but they do not believe their attorneys are capable of being so helpful. This is an accurate perception in some cases. However, there is much that determined administrators can do to improve agency legal representation. Chapter 5, *Improving Agency Legal Representation*, identifies steps that can be taken by administrators for this purpose.

Use of Paralegals or Other Specialized Staff

One key to effective work with the courts can be the use of specialized paralegal staff for certain court related functions. Specialized staff can both help the agency get better results in court and help smooth agency-court relations.

General Strategies for Working with Courts

For example, many courts have concerns that agency staff members do not conduct sufficient searches for missing parents. There must be sufficient proof of a diligent search to satisfy legal requirements. While the task of conducting the search always must remain partly the responsibility of the case manager, in a large office it is logical to assign certain search responsibilities to specially trained clerical staff.

Clerical staff can contact the child support agency to:

* check for further information;

* mail out a standard set of forms to the departments of motor vehicles, vital statistics, etc.;

* help prepare the affidavit for court; and

* take other routine steps.

Generally speaking, using clerical staff for searches is both more efficient and more cost effective than leaving these tasks entirely to caseworkers.

In many places, paralegal workers are used for a broad range of court preparation activities. These workers may be employed by the agency or by the agency's attorneys. In either case, they need to work closely with both workers and attorneys. Their job is to allow the attorneys to focus on more complex matters by helping caseworkers make cases ready for court.

Some possible tasks of paralegal workers (sometimes referred to as *court liaisons*) are as follows:

* They can help prepare and review forms the agency submits to the court.

* They can help the caseworker put together a packet of materials for the attorney (e.g., proposed witness lists, medical reports, birth certificates, case narratives) in difficult cases like those involving a contested termination of parental rights.

* They can help contact witnesses to inform them of the court date and can make sure needed subpoenas have been issued.

❖ They can answer routine questions for caseworkers concerning the completeness of their investigation or preparation prior to court.

If former caseworkers are used in this capacity, they can perform a broader range of functions, including providing casework advice for difficult cases. Some caseworkers have a flair for forensics and enjoy this type of work.

For example, some agencies in rural areas have roving specialists to assist in cases where children are unable to return to a parent and termination of parental rights or guardianship is being considered. Because termination cases do not happen every week in rural areas, such a specialist may be needed. They can serve as a casework consultant, as well as a paralegal, helping the caseworker decide whether to go forward with the case.

Another interesting possible use of paralegal staff is to help resolve interagency conflicts or misunderstandings. For example, paralegals can be used as liaisons between the child welfare agency and other agencies within the Executive Department to coordinate interagency meetings on difficult cases and develop interagency protocols.

Appeals

Another important strategy in working with your court is the occasional appeal from adverse decisions by judges. If your agency never appeals, you are probably not receiving complete legal representation. Appeals from adverse judicial decisions are expensive and time consuming, but are an essential tool in dealing with courts.

When to Appeal Adverse Cases

The decision to appeal an adverse decision cannot be made lightly. Appeals are expensive, often costing thousands of dollars. Although many states have taken steps to expedite appeals, the process tends to be slow. In some places, an appeal usually will take six months to complete. In other places, the typical appeal will take 18 months. Obviously, the issues at stake in an adverse decision must be important to the agency and there must be a reasonable likelihood of success.

In most cases, agencies decide to appeal in order to set a favorable precedent, often when the agency has an ongoing disagreement with the court and hopes that success on appeal will resolve the disagreement in the agency's favor. For example, an agency might decide to appeal if the court repeatedly refuses to terminate parental rights in a particular type of case where the agency feels there is a legal basis for termination. Another agency might decide to appeal if the court routinely orders children to be placed in a setting the agency deems inappropriate.

Occasionally, however, the agency appeals simply because it believes a court's decision in a specific case may be disastrous to a child. Such an appeal might occur, for example, where the court orders a child to be returned to a family but the agency believes the child will be in great danger. Because the agency cannot appeal every case in which it disagrees with the judge, these kinds of appeals occur in unusual and extreme situations.

Some agencies have decided never to appeal because doing so may anger the judge. Assuming the agency has competent legal representation, this attitude is counterproductive. Appeals are a professional and appropriate way to gain clarity on a legal issue and are not offensive to most judges. On the other hand, if your judge is unusually domineering, the best strategy is not to be overly placating.

It is true that most judges do not like being appealed, but an occasional appeal is needed to gain the judge's respect. If only parents' attorneys appeal, your judge may feel tempted to reduce the risk of being overturned on appeal by ruling in the parents' favor on difficult issues. The judge should be equally concerned that the agency may appeal.

Of course, there are reasons to be careful about bringing appeals — besides the cost involved and the chances of success. Sometimes agencies file appeals out of anger or frustration. This tactic can be counterproductive, because unsuccessful appeals can backfire and appeals are often not the best instrument to address problems between courts and agencies.

Each appeal needs to be carefully crafted to correct judicial decisions that are harmful to children. If an appeal is not likely to accomplish this goal, conciliation and negotiation with the judge may be a better approach.

Attorneys Who Do Not Want to Appeal

Some agencies' attorneys are chronically reluctant to appeal. Certainly, an agency needs to rely on the technical advice of its attorneys in deciding whether to appeal, but if the agency is repeatedly losing important cases and the attorney never wants to appeal, something is amiss.

Attorneys may avoid appeals for reasons unrelated to the merits of the case. For an inexperienced attorney, handling an appeal is a daunting process, involving the preparation and submission of a scholarly, written legal argument (*brief*). Preparation of appeals is especially time consuming and is sometimes threatening to attorneys who have not handled many appeals in the past.

With many attorneys, once the first appeal is taken, the barrier is overcome and there is less resistance in the future. As an attorney gains experience, appeals become less time-consuming, especially now that computers can be used to ease the process of brief writing. Certain "boilerplate" arguments in child welfare cases can be adapted from one brief to another.

In some states, different attorneys handle appeals for the agency than those who routinely appear in court for the agency. In such states, the agency can get an expert impartial assessment of its chances of winning an appeal. A case's chances on appeal depend, in large part, upon whether the trial attorney did a good job at trial ("made a good record for appeal").

If attorneys habitually decline to pursue appeals, an agency may have several options. If the agency's attorneys are locally based but not hired by the local agency (e.g., employed by the county or district attorney), the agency may be able to look to the state for assistance. In some states where routine legal representation of child welfare agencies is provided locally, state government does provide legal assistance for difficult cases and appeals. If the state doesn't provide this kind of assistance, the agency should consider trying to get the state to provide such assistance in the future.

If the agency hires its own attorneys and they always refuse to appeal, the agency may need to change attorneys. Likewise, if the agency contracts with attorneys who refuse to appeal, it may need to contract with new attorneys.

A most difficult situation occurs when an agency is represented exclusively by a local prosecutor or county attorney who refuses to appeal. In this situation, the agency must try to negotiate with that attorney. If negotiation is unsuccessful, the agency may want to develop a long-range strategy to obtain permission to hire its own attorneys.

To accomplish this goal, the child welfare agency must make a convincing case to the county board or state legislature (whichever is applicable) that its current legal representation needs improvement (e.g., greater specialization, added staff). The agency must also show that what it proposes is cost effective.

Planning for Appeals

Sometimes, when agencies are concerned about a specific ongoing disagreement with their courts, it is helpful to prepare a "test case" that is likely to be appealed. There are two main things an attorney does to set up a case for appeal:

❖ whatever legal issue is to be argued on appeal is clearly presented to the trial judge (otherwise it can't brought up during the appeal), and

❖ the evidence is very strong so that legal issue to be argued on appeal will not be confused by weak or conflicting facts.

The following example shows how a test case can come about:

> The Department of Children's Services in County W feels that it should not have to make efforts to rehabilitate severely mentally ill parents under ASFA when the parents have had already received years of unsuccessful mental health treatment and can be considered chronic abusers.
>
> The Department is frustrated that its juvenile court judge consistently requires the Department to develop case plans to try to rehabilitate such parents, when the Department wants to legally free the children for adoption (terminate parental rights) without delay.
>
> The Department's attorney says that state law is not entirely clear, but there is a good legal argument that the judge is interpreting the termination of parental rights law too strictly in these cases. Therefore, the Department has decided to prepare a test case to try to create a

legal precedent that will allow the Department to seek early permanent placements of children with hopelessly mentally ill parents.

The Department has selected a particularly clear cut case involving a three-year-old child whose parents have repeatedly abused her, are severely schizophrenic, and have long histories of institutionalization and treatment. They are considered by mental health experts to have very poor prognoses for improvement. In addition, there are no relatives available to care for the child and it seems clear that the best plan is adoption.

The Department will not follow its usual practice of developing an obviously futile case plan to satisfy the judge. Instead, the Department is about to file a petition to terminate parental rights.

To prepare its case, the Department has arranged psychological examinations of the parents and child by top professionals, including a professor of psychiatry from the local medical school. The Department has assembled a detailed psychiatric history describing prior treatment of the parents.

The Department's expert witnesses are prepared to testify emphatically that the parents are unlikely to improve enough in the near future to enable them to care for the child. Further, the agency has identified numerous witnesses who can offer exhaustive and vivid testimony demonstrating the aberrant behavior of the parents and their poor care of the child.

If the Department loses the case and needs to appeal, its attorneys will be able to present the court with a case involving clear cut evidence showing that the parents are unlikely to improve due to their mental illness. Given this evidence, the case can set the legal precedent that, in cases involving mentally ill parents unlikely to improve, trial judges should terminate parental rights without forcing the agency to implement a futile case plan for the parents.

It is possible, of course, that the judge will surprise the Department and rule in its favor, eliminating the possibility of appeal. Even if that happens, however, the agency's exceptionally strong case may have convinced the judge to take a different view in the future toward cases involving severely mentally ill parents. If the case helped to change the judge's mind without the necessity to appeal either in this case or in future cases, that would be the best result of all.

Legal Basis for Appeals

To win an appeal, the agency's attorney must convince the appellate court that the trial judge made an error that changed the outcome of the case. There are numerous types of possible legal errors. One common type of error asserted in appeals of child welfare cases is that the judge is misinterpreting state law governing when the state can infringe on parental rights. For example, the agency may argue in an appeal that the judge is misinterpreting state law concerning:

❖ when the agency can remove a child from home,

❖ when a child must be returned home, or

❖ the grounds for the termination of parental rights.

The judge misinterpreted state law. In the example described above, assume that the Department does lose the original trial because of the judge's strict interpretation of the state's grounds for the termination of parental rights. The Department would argue in its appeal that the judge's legal error was his misinterpretation of the state statute's grounds for the termination of parental rights.

The judge exceeded his or her judicial authority. Another important, but less common, legal basis for agency appeals in child welfare cases is that the judge has erred by overstepping his or her powers in ordering the agency to do something. For example, agencies have claimed that judges exceeded their powers when ordering a child to be placed in a specific foster home supervised by the agency, when ordering the agency to send a parent to a particular service provider, and when ordering a child to be sent to a particularly expensive out-of-state institution.

The success of such appeals depends upon the powers of juvenile courts under state law. Results vary. There are great differences in the powers of juvenile courts in different states.

There was insufficient evidence to support the judge's decision. Another important basis for appeal in a child welfare case is that there was a lack of evidence to back up the judge's ruling. In other words, the error is not that the judge misinterpreted the law, but rather that the judge's ruling was contrary to the evidence.

This argument might be made in the above case involving a mentally ill parent if the judge's decision were slightly different. Suppose that the judge conceded that the law allows immediate termination of parental rights (without implementing a case plan) when parents have a mental illness that makes them unable to care for their children and there is little hope of improvement.

However, suppose further that in this case, the judge found there was a good chance the parents might improve. If that were the judge's ruling, the judicial error asserted in the appeal would have to be that the judge disregarded overwhelming evidence.

An agency might also argue on appeal that a judge's decision was contrary to the evidence and in essence that the judge has "practiced social work from the bench." For example, suppose a judge believes that a particular psychiatrist, Dr. Smith, is especially effective in treating sexually abused children.

The judge orders a particular child to be sent to Dr. Smith, although there is no evidence presented in court demonstrating that another psychiatrist could not do equally well. Even assuming that state law gives the judge the power to order that an abused child is to be treated by a specific psychiatrist when there is evidence to support the order, in this case there was no such evidence.

Appeals challenging "social work from the bench" are not common, perhaps partly because the issue in dispute usually will no longer exist by the time the appellate court makes a decision. However, in some cases, it may be possible to delay enforcement of (*stay*) the judge's order while the case is on appeal.

Even if the court's order will remain in effect during the long appeal, the case may establish important precedent for later cases.

There are many technical procedural issues in pursuing an appeal, and some states make it easier than others to challenge "social work from the bench." Of course, the kinds of issues that may be appealed vary greatly from state to state.

3

Important Issues for Court and Agency Collaboration

> I knew things weren't right between us and our courts, but I hadn't really taken time to identify the problems or to figure out strategies to solve them.

This chapter discusses in greater depth how to deal with specific issues frequently arising between agencies and courts. Strategies for addressing each issue are suggested.

Improving Compliance with Federal Child Welfare Law

Child welfare agencies cannot fully satisfy the requirements of ASFA and its implementing regulations without the cooperation of the courts. Several parts of ASFA call upon courts to perform specific steps in cases involving maltreated children within shorter time frames than ever before. If the courts do not take such steps, child welfare agencies may fail federal reviews and lose federal funding.

Specifically, in order for agencies to be eligible for certain federal funds, ASFA requires that:

> Courts determine whether "continuation in the home is contrary to the welfare of the child" or "placement would be in the best interest of the child" in the first court order issued after the child's removal from the home;

Courts determine whether the child welfare agency has made "reasonable efforts" to prevent removal of each foster child, within 60 days of the child's actual removal from the home, or that a lack of efforts is reasonable under certain circumstances;

Courts determine whether the child welfare agency has made reasonable efforts to finalize a permanency plan within 12 months of the child's removal;

Courts consider the views of the child welfare agency if deciding the child's placement;

Courts (or appropriate administrative body) conduct a review of the child's status at least every six months;

Courts explicitly extend a "trial home visit" that lasts longer than six months or the time previously set by the court; and

Courts meet the same requirements for delinquents and status offenders placed in foster care as those for dependent children.

See 42 U.S.C. §§ 620-632, 670-679; 45 C.F.R. §§ 1356.21(c); 1356.21(b); 1356.21(g); 1356.21(e). For a complete discussion of ASFA's requirements, see D. Ratterman Baker, et al., *Making Sense of the ASFA Regulations: A Roadmap for Effective Implementation* (ABA 2001).

In passing ASFA, Congress amended the federal foster care law to make safety and permanency the focal point of the law and continued to recognize the courts' essential role in achieving permanence for abused and neglected children. Congress recognized the courts' key decision-making role in child welfare cases and challenged courts and agencies to achieve permanency for children in a timely fashion.

Many agencies have persistent difficulty in persuading courts to meet these requirements. Some judges refuse to make required findings. Others do not make the findings in every case or fail to do so consistently within federal time limits. These problems are not necessarily due to judicial hostility toward agencies, judicial disinterest, or judicial uncooperativeness, and there are concrete steps agencies can take to identify and resolve the problems presented.

10 Basic Steps to Improve Compliance

Before discussing how agency administrators can persuade courts to implement any specific ASFA provisions, it is helpful to consider some generic strategies. The following are 10 steps administrators should take to improve judicial compliance with all of the above requirements:

Find out why judges are not complying. Agencies need to find out exactly why judges are not implementing federal requirements. To discover the barriers to judicial compliance, agencies need to use their best social work skills to interview judges and other court officials.

There are a number of common reasons why some judges do not consistently comply with ASFA. To begin with, there is the fundamental fact that, unlike child welfare agencies, the courts have no financial stake in compliance with ASFA; courts have nothing directly to gain or lose from the agency's passing or failing the federal reviews.

Besides the lack of financial incentives, judges may be reluctant to implement ASFA for one or more of the following reasons:

❖ Judges do not understand the reasons behind ASFA's requirements;

❖ Judges do not agree with ASFA's requirements;

❖ Judges receive inconsistent or unclear messages concerning exactly what they are supposed to do to comply with ASFA;

❖ Judges feel agencies are asking them to comply in a manner that amounts to an empty exercise, i.e., by putting meaningless words onto a form;

❖ Judges feel agencies are asking them to make findings when the agencies do not present evidence to support the findings;

❖ Juvenile courts are overwhelmed and judges feel they do not have time to comply with ASFA; and

❖ Judges believe state and federal law does not require them to implement ASFA.

Sometimes, even when judges are inclined to comply with federal requirements, weaknesses in court procedure, staffing, or organization can be a barrier. For example, judges might find it difficult to consistently remember to make "reasonable efforts" determinations if they do not use court forms with a blank for reasonable efforts.

They may even forget to fill out the reasonable efforts blank in the form and may need the help of court staff to remember. Yet, the court may not have enough clerical staff to help, or the clerical help may not be trained to check files for ASFA compliance.

Thus, the first step to improve judicial compliance, before trying to suggest solutions or to offer help, is to study and understand the precise reasons for noncompliance — if possible, with the assistance of agency attorneys.

Make sure agency employees are thoroughly familiar with ASFA. After identifying the reasons for judicial noncompliance, make sure agency employees themselves are thoroughly grounded in the requirements of ASFA before permitting them to go to speak with the judge. Many judges complain that agencies haven't been able to really explain what the law requires and why.

For example, if the agency tells the judge, "We don't know why the federal government is insisting on this," the court will not be eager to cooperate. Nor will the judge be very inclined to cooperate when the agency cannot explain the fine points of ASFA.

Keep your lawyer actively involved. Besides making sure agency employees have a thorough understanding of what federal law requires before approaching the judge, insist that the agency lawyer be actively involved in preparing for and participating in meetings with the court. Make sure the agency lawyer takes enough time to master the relevant ASFA provisions and spends time instructing the group of people going to meet the judge.

The agency lawyer's familiarity with ASFA should extend to the statute itself, federal regulations, all relevant written federal policy statements, state law implementing the federal requirements, and relevant portions of the agency policy manual. The lawyer should be prepared to explain the purpose of each requirement. To gain familiarity with ASFA, attorneys can refer to a number of source materials which are listed in the bibliography. The lawyer should also be provided with relevant federal policy interpretations. (Every state child welfare agency and regional federal office of the Department of Health and Human Services should have a full set of federal interpretations of ASFA.)

Give definitive written answers to judges' questions about ASFA.
When judges ask for technical interpretations of ASFA, make sure that your agency gives clear, definitive, and authoritative answers. Judges become very frustrated when they receive inconsistent answers to questions or discover that prior answers were inaccurate. To make sure that the agency is answering questions consistently and correctly on a statewide basis, the following steps will help:

- Identify the agency "expert" on ASFA's requirements and give the expert's name, address, and telephone number to juvenile court judges throughout the state.

- Let the judges know the expert will give prompt written answers to any questions upon request.

- Make sure the expert is well trained in ASFA's requirements.

- Preferably, the expert should be an attorney; if not, make sure that the expert has liberal access to an agency attorney who also is well schooled in ASFA.

- If a question requires federal policy clarification, insist on a written answer from the regional or national office of the Children's Bureau, United States Department of Health and Human Services. Be persistent.

❖ If you are unable to get timely written answers to questions (whether arising within the agency or from judges), send confirming letters concerning oral answers and politely renew the request for a written answer. Besides helping you to deal with judges, this step helps protect against federal reviewers penalizing the agency for following federal instructions that were given only verbally.

❖ To explain the basis of your answers to judges or lawyers, send them copies of pertinent letters and written policies from the federal government, especially if there has been a change in federal law or policy. In addition to being helpful, it will document the accuracy of your prior statements and show that the state agency is not being inconsistent.

Have your attorney review your letters to the courts. Before you send out correspondence to the courts — especially when you are proposing procedures, explaining the law, or suggesting the use of forms — ask your lawyer to review the correspondence in advance. If the lawyer does not seem to be paying close attention to the correspondence, ask specific questions such as whether the agency has interpreted federal requirements correctly or whether your proposal makes sense in terms of existing juvenile court procedure.

Lawyers can help sharpen your correspondence not only by ensuring its legal accuracy, but also by using proper legal terminology. Judges are used to receiving information presented in a certain way, and they are more persuaded when this occurs. Lawyers and judges are exacting about the use of proper legal terminology.

Send brief correspondence with any background material attached. When communicating to the judge concerning ASFA, make sure the memorandum or letter is brief. Judges receive enormous amounts of written information, and it is important to keep correspondence as short and to the point as possible.

Attaching background material to the memorandum or letter can add both precision and credibility to the agency's message — if the material is exactly on point. Helpful background material might include excerpts from the pertinent federal statutes, federal policy interpretations, and state statutes.

In some cases, it will be appropriate also to enclose brief and pertinent excerpts from relevant state regulations or sections of the state policy manual.

The agency should not be overly concerned that most judges will not carefully review the attached background material. Some judges probably will review the attachments carefully, some will file them away for future reference, and some will be impressed with the attachments, although they do not have time to read them.

Let judges know you support ASFA. When courts implement ASFA *properly*, children, families, and agencies benefit. Rights are protected, errors are avoided, and permanency for children is accelerated. Superficial compliance is not a desirable goal for the agency.

It is important to tell the judge that the agency believes in ASFA and it wants the court to comply with both the letter and spirit of the law. Let the judge know the agency wants to help the judge fulfill the law. For example, tell the judge the agency wants a meaningful reasonable efforts determination and a thorough and decisive permanency hearing.

It is ultimately self-defeating to tell the judge that ASFA's requirements are meaningless and the agency just wants to fulfill federal technicalities in order to be able to draw funding. While many judges do have sympathy for the agency's need for funding, most never feel right about complying with what they regard as meaningless federal technicalities. Agencies denigrating ASFA usually have great difficulty obtaining consistent judicial cooperation.

Be as helpful as possible to the judge. Be prepared to explain what the agency is willing to do to assist the judge to make the findings required by federal law. The following are some things you might want to offer to do to help:

- Offer to make changes in your own forms, if necessary.

- Offer to instruct your lawyers to present evidence in support of the findings required by federal law (e.g., *contrary to the welfare* and *reasonable efforts*).

- ❖ Offer to instruct your caseworkers to prepare testimony in support of findings.

- ❖ Offer to use your own staff to help keep tabs on compliance and to bring any problems to the court staff's attention.

- ❖ Urge the judge to bring any procedural problems to your attention and promise to act on them expeditiously.

- ❖ Urge the judge to bring any problems with particular personnel to your attention, such as caseworkers who do not prepare testimony in support of the findings.

- ❖ Promise to take the judge's problems and findings very seriously — e.g., promise to review all negative reasonable efforts findings and to try to quickly correct problems referred to in the findings.

- ❖ Promise to let the judge know how you respond to his or her requests, recommendations, or orders.

By making such offers and commitments, do not think you are allowing the judge to "take over" the agency. Rather, you are showing the court that you value its judicial monitoring function. You are giving the court the message that when the judge brings matters to your attention you will want to correct the problem or at least take the opportunity to explain to the judge how the agency works and why.

Support state legislation fully implementing ASFA. Most states have adopted detailed state legislation implementing ASFA. It is more likely that your state now needs clarifying amendments to clear up confusion or inconsistencies. If possible, work with juvenile court judges and private child advocacy organizations to help improve your statute.

Well-written state legislation represents a mandatory and undebatable directive to judges that they must comply with ASFA's requirements. Furthermore, with state law requiring compliance with ASFA, it is much easier to persuade appellate courts and court administrators to amend their court forms to comply with the federal law.

Beyond mere compliance, enacting and amending state legislation is an opportunity to go beyond the bare language of the federal requirements and to implement their spirit. It can be a way to improve the quality of the juvenile court process.

Try to persuade the courts to adopt forms that call upon judges to make findings in compliance with ASFA. Court forms are probably the single most effective means to avoid failing federal reviews. Often courts implement the spirit of federal requirements, e.g., experienced judges hear evidence of the agency's efforts to preserve the family and conduct thorough and searching periodic case reviews.

Yet, when these judges do not use court forms that set forth the ASFA requirements, they may not make the findings required by federal law. Thus, without court forms tracking ASFA requirements, it is difficult to comply even in a strong court. Of course, there are good and bad forms. Forms should be designed to reinforce good judicial practice rather than to induce the judge to approve of agency actions without reflection. Later sections of this chapter discuss the pernicious impact of bad forms and suggest what to include in forms designed to comply with particular federal requirements.

To persuade courts to use forms tracking ASFA requirements, you may choose to approach the courts on the state or local levels. Check with your attorneys to identify who in the judiciary should be contacted. The following are some possible people to approach concerning the adoption of court forms:

❖ **The state's Administrative Office of the Courts.**

> The Administrative Office of the Courts (AOC) is the statewide court administrator, who normally reports to the Chief Justice of the State's highest court. In many states, this office promulgates court forms.

❖ **The relevant Court Rules Committee.**

> In states with juvenile court rules, the committee responsible for the drafting of such rules may be a good place to go to propose the adoption of forms. Note, however, that court rules are usually developed very

slowly, so you may not want to have the court rules require a specific form.

Federal requirements change from time to time, and it may take too long to get the committee's approval to change the state form. Instead, it may be better to ask the rules committee to:

- ❖ require, by court rule, that court forms include findings mandated by the federal law, such as "reasonable efforts";
- ❖ require the courts to use forms approved by the AOC or to use alternatives approved by the AOC; and
- ❖ direct the AOC to approve local forms only if they include at least all of the information called for in the AOC-approved form.

❖ **The state juvenile and family court judges organization or its president.**

In many states, the juvenile and family court judges association takes a strong leadership role on issues concerning the juvenile courts. The association may prefer to develop suggested forms that individual judges can choose whether to adopt. On the other hand, the association may support efforts for the development of forms by the AOC or juvenile court rules committee.

In most states, the AOC relies on the recommendations both of individual juvenile judges and their association concerning court forms for juvenile court. Likewise, the juvenile court rules committees have juvenile court judges as members and also take the comments of other judges strongly into account.

❖ **The state Court Improvement Project.** In 1993, Congress provided federal grant funds to improve how courts handle child abuse and neglect cases. State Court Improvement Projects are currently funded through September 2006. Each state determines how to use its funds, usually in conjunction with a court improvement committee or task force. The state Court Improvement Project may be willing to develop and pilot forms with the assistance of the agency.

❖ **The county or district attorneys' association.**

In some states, county or district attorneys represent the public child welfare agency in juvenile court. Within the state organization of county or district attorneys, there usually is a committee or subcommittee that focuses on juvenile and family issues. It is important to be aware of and work with such committees.

You may be able to work with the county or district attorneys to persuade them to use forms that assist you to comply with federal requirements. For example, in some courts, the county or district attorneys actually draw up orders and findings for the court. Thus, when submitting orders, if they were to use forms complying with ASFA, federal law would be satisfied.

In addition, the county or district attorneys may play a prominent role in the preparation of rules and the approval of forms for the juvenile courts. They typically participate in court rules committees and their comments are taken into account in the development of court forms. Thus, as with the juvenile court judges association, it is important to work with the organization of county or district attorneys.

❖ **The child welfare agency's attorney(s).**

Of course, if a child welfare agency has its own attorneys, they should be assisting the agency through the entire process of trying to develop forms for the court. For example, if local attorneys handle cases in juvenile court, the agency's own attorney should be helping the agency deal with the association of county or district attorneys, the AOC, the juvenile court rules committee, or any others in the legal system.

Strategies to Persuade Judges to Make Judicial Determinations

As a condition for the payment of federal matching funds for each child in foster care, ASFA requires that the court make certain determinations. First, the court must determine that "continuation in the home is contrary to the welfare of the child, or that placement would be in the best interest of the child" in the *first* court order made on the child's removal, even if removal is temporary. 45 C.F.R. § 1356.21(c). In addition, within 60 days of the child's actual removal, the court must find that "reasonable efforts have been made to prevent the child's removal from home." Within 12 months of removal, the court must determine that the agency has made reasonable efforts to finalize a permanency plan, whether for reunification or a new permanent placement. 45 C.F.R. § 1356.21(d).

Contrary to the Welfare. The ASFA regulations provide specific guidance on how to make a *contrary to the welfare* finding and what to include in such a finding. The contrary to the welfare finding must be made in the *first* court order that removes the child from the home either physically or constructively, whether an emergency or non-emergency order. Failure to document this finding makes the child ineligible for federal funding for the duration of that stay in foster care.

Judges do not have to use the specific term *contrary to the welfare* in the order. However, the court must indicate whether the child remaining in the home would the contrary to the welfare of the child and/or that it is in the best interests of the child to be removed from the home. The order should indicate how the court arrived at its conclusion.

This individualized determination can be made by referencing materials such as a court report, psychological report, or sustained petition. A checklist is acceptable as long as the state can demonstrate that the findings were made on an individual review of the child's specific circumstances.

Obtaining *contrary to the welfare* findings can be challenging in states that claim foster care reimbursements for delinquent children. Unlike child abuse and neglect cases, courts in delinquency cases often do not make such determinations when children are first removed from home. When children are initially removed, it is often for temporary pretrial detention rather than foster placement.

Also, for example, a child may be removed from home for the purpose of incarceration based upon findings that the child committed a certain number of offenses. In such cases, it may be difficult to convince judges to make findings to the effect that the placement is necessary for the welfare of the child when a child is first placed in detention. The court may have no information regarding the welfare of the child at the time of detention, and know only that the child has committed an offense.

On the other hand, there are many situations involving delinquent children removed from home for the first time in which judges can honestly determine that removal is necessary for the child's welfare as well as due to the child's commission of an offense.

For example, if a probation officer has been working with a child and believes that a foster or group home will provide better supervision and prevent further delinquency, a judge can make a good faith finding that continuation in the home would be contrary to the child's best interests. Likewise, the judge can determine whether the relevant agency (including the probation officer) has made reasonable efforts to try to prevent the need for removal.

Reasonable Efforts. In order for the state to be eligible for federal foster care matching funds, ASFA requires that a court has found that there have been reasonable efforts to prevent placement and reasonable efforts to finalize a permanency plan. For a thorough discussion of reasonable efforts to finalize permanency plans, see C. Fiermonte and J. Renne, *Making It Permanent: Reasonable Efforts to Finalize Permanency Plans* (ABA 2002). Reasonable efforts findings are not required, however, in certain statutorily defined circumstances, e.g., when certain felonies have been committed by the parent, parental rights to another child have been terminated, or "aggravated circumstances" as defined by state law are present.

Reasonable efforts findings should be detailed and include specific relevant findings about the case. Courts can describe the reasonable efforts in a court order, cross reference agency or court reports, cross reference a sustained petition, and/or utilize a detailed checklist.

It is important to understand why some courts are not interested in the reasonable efforts findings and why some judges prefer to make perfunctory findings. Some of the reasons for both are as follows:

❖ They want the agency to receive its federal funds.

- ❖ They believe making negative reasonable efforts findings where agency services are deficient only makes the funding situation worse.

- ❖ Their courts are overwhelmed by growing caseloads and other demands and they feel they do not have time to look into the agency's efforts to assist the family.

- ❖ They feel the reasonable efforts determination is irrelevant to their real decisions in the case.

- ❖ They feel there is no point in reviewing reasonable efforts because it won't change anything.

- ❖ They are uncomfortable making negative findings that may give offense to caseworkers.

- ❖ They feel they don't know much about the agency and have no objective basis upon which to make reasonable efforts findings.

That many agency administrators want to obtain meaningless reasonable efforts findings is understandable. There is a natural tension between agencies and courts, and real judicial oversight of reasonable efforts sometimes is uncomfortable to workers. Workers therefore complain about the court to supervisors and administrators.

Further, meaningless but consistent findings would mean more secure funding for the agency. Finally, some judges cannot or will not do a good job of reviewing reasonable efforts.

On the other hand, administrators often fail to realize all that can be gained by meaningful judicial oversight of reasonable efforts. First, such oversight really can correct weaknesses in agency performance or alert administrators as to what weaknesses need to be corrected.

Second, the review of reasonable efforts can speed permanency planning, i.e., where the judge explicitly approves what the agency has been doing to preserve the family and makes a clear record to that effect. The judge's approval communicates to the family the importance of cooperation with the agency. The judge's written decision, especially if it includes detailed findings of fact, provides a record that will be invaluable if the agency later needs to terminate parental rights.

In many places, trying to persuade courts to make meaningless reasonable efforts findings has turned out to be an unsound funding strategy. Judges who are unwilling to examine reasonable efforts often are uncomfortable making perfunctory findings and simply make no finding. It is often easier to help them make a meaningful finding than no finding at all. In fact, agencies really do not risk a substantial loss of funds when judges rigorously review reasonable efforts. With rare exceptions, judges who thoroughly review reasonable efforts make positive findings in the vast majority of cases.

Furthermore, as the result of ASFA, increasing numbers of judges do insist that agencies present evidence in order to obtain positive findings. Agencies that face such judges must actually document and present to the judge what their efforts have been to preserve the family. Agencies must revise their own forms for that purpose, train their caseworkers, and gain the cooperation of their attorneys.

As always, to persuade the judge to cooperate, you want to explain to the judge how you will help. To assist with the reasonable efforts findings, offer to provide the judge with better information about reasonable efforts in each case. As explained above, this might be done by inserting a description of the agency's efforts in agency court reports or by developing a separate form to describe the agency's reasonable efforts. Some courts actually require a separate "affidavit of efforts" to be filed in support of the reasonable efforts finding.

Explain to the judges that you are seeking their assistance to improve decision making for children as well as to get funding. Explain that you regard their oversight of reasonable efforts as important and helpful to the agency and to the children and families which it serves. Tell them you will take their observations and criticisms very seriously.

Let judges know you value early oversight of reasonable efforts because it allows the agency to correct problems early rather than, for example, losing at the termination of parental rights stage and having to start over. In fact, you should encourage the court to make reasonable efforts findings before they are due.

This practice will allow you to address the court's concerns before losing federal funding and reduces noncompliance. For example, if the agency seeks a finding of reasonable efforts to prevent placement and the judge needs more information, the agency will need time to gather and present the additional information.

Similarly, if the judge finds there were not reasonable efforts to finalize a permanent home, the agency will have time to fix the problem before the deadline runs. To reduce the potential loss of federal funds, you should seek to correct any problem resulting from a missing or negative finding and request a special hearing to obtain a positive finding.

Assuming that your agency actually values the reasonable efforts determination, i.e., wants judges to conduct a meaningful inquiry concerning your efforts to preserve the family, using the *right* court forms can make a big difference. The best approach is to use a form that includes a blank for the court to describe the agency's efforts to assist the family. The judge can either fill in the blank with his or her description of the services provided or can cross reference to information provided in the agency's report.

The advantage of this approach is that before the judge fills in the blank, he or she must listen to and think about what the agency has done to help the family. In turn, the judge must require the agency attorney and caseworker to provide information on the topic. This then requires the caseworker to do the casework that will be necessary to satisfy the judge. In addition, the description of the agency's efforts provides a tactically valuable record of what the agency has done to help the family. This description will be reviewed by the judge (or subsequent judges) prior to future court hearings.

Another important element of agency strategy is how to react to adverse reasonable efforts findings. The same strategy applies whether the judge explicitly makes a negative finding, states that more needs to happen before a positive finding is made, or simply does not make a finding.

If the judge's concern seems legitimate, the best approach is to try to correct the problem and bring the case back to court as soon as possible. If the nature of the judge's objection is unclear, the best approach is to return to court as soon as possible to find out.

In order to respond properly to adverse findings, several agency policies are needed:

❖ First, all adverse findings should promptly be reported to supervisors and managers.

❖ Second, attorneys should be asked to return to court as soon as practical, to try to obtain a positive finding.

❖ Third, caseworkers should be expected promptly to correct the problems causing the adverse determination, if consistent with agency policy.

❖ Fourth, administrators should be made aware of patterns in adverse determinations and be expected to try to correct them.

Most agencies adopting such policies have been able to correct adverse determinations rapidly in the great majority of cases, thereby minimizing the loss of federal matching funds.

A final element of strategy to obtain positive reasonable efforts findings is to clarify when the lack of services to preserve or rehabilitate the family are reasonable. In other words, even if there is no applicable exception to the requirement to make reasonable efforts, e.g., *aggravated circumstances*, it may be that a lack of efforts is reasonable after assessing a family.

If, in a specific case, the goal is not to return the child home and if the agency has initiated proceedings to legally free the child for adoption or permanent guardianship, a lack of reunification services should be deemed reasonable. It is very important that agency workers be aware of the types of circumstances when early termination of parental rights rather than clearly futile or unsafe *reasonable efforts* should be considered.

Agencies should develop a realistic procedure to consider these cases so that futile cases do not disproportionately drain resources.

Strategies to Persuade Judges to Consider the Agency's Views When Deciding the Child's Placement

ASFA specifies that the placement and care of a child in foster care is the responsibility of an appropriate public agency. 42 U.S.C. § 672(a)(2). Federal regulations state that, if the court orders placement in a specific foster care placement without allowing the agency and parties to present evidence and argument regarding the placement, the state cannot receive matching federal funds.

The rationale behind this requirement is to prevent the court from taking responsibility for the placement and care of the child away from the child welfare agency. However, this regulation does not mean that the court must always agree with the agency's recommendations; rather, the court must hear testimony on the issue and consider the agency's viewpoint.

If judges in your jurisdiction are used to making unilateral decisions regarding placement, you will need to be tactful and well prepared in presenting testimony that supports your agency's recommendations. In most instances, however, judges will appreciate more detailed information regarding the recommended placement.

While this regulation does not guarantee judicial approval of your recommendation in every case, with proper education and solid presentations, you can avoid unilateral decisions that may result in needlessly expensive and restrictive placements.

Strategies to Persuade Judges to Conduct Valid Six-Month Reviews

Federal law requires that at least once every six months there must be a review of every case involving a child in state supervised foster care. This review may be conducted by a court, agency panel, or panel of citizen volunteers.

Whatever the form of review (including court review), at its conclusion several issues must be explicitly addressed. These issues include:

- ❖ the safety of the child;

- ❖ the appropriateness and continuing need for the child's placement;

- ❖ the extent of compliance with the case plan;

- ❖ the extent of progress that has been made to remedy the problems causing the child to be in foster care; and

- ❖ a projected date by which the child may be returned home or placed for adoption or legal guardianship. 42 U.S.C. § 675(5)(B).

Congress intended that the above issues actually would be addressed in the course of a six-month review, whether the review is conducted by a court or administrative body. Because of the separation of powers and the legal independence of judges, it is not easy to achieve consistent compliance with federal six-month review requirements through court hearings.

Unlike other federal foster care requirements applicable to the courts, agencies can comply with the six-month review requirement on their own. Agencies having great difficulty persuading courts to fulfill six-month review requirements should seriously consider conducting six-month reviews themselves.

Some agencies opting for administrative six-month reviews stagger the timing of agency and court reviews. For example, in one county, the court reviews each case roughly six and 12 months after placement. The agency reviews each case roughly three and nine months after placement.

If you are in a state where courts conduct frequent reviews, yet your agency decides it must conduct its own six-month reviews for compliance purposes, administrators should carefully explain their reasons for doing so to the juvenile court judges, the AOC, and others. Administrators should explain that federal law:

- ❖ demands specific types of determinations be made in every six-month review, and

- ❖ does not permit delays beyond six months, even in cases where there is a reasonable justification for a hearing set-over or continuance.

It helps if you also explain to the courts that you view court reviews as valuable, and you plan for your reviews to be complementary. That is, you might want to explain that you believe there is value to staggered court and agency reviews. The argument goes something like this: Court reviews help keep the agency accountable, and agency reviews reinforce compliance with court orders and help maintain internal quality control.

Strategies to Persuade Judges to Conduct Valid Permanency Hearings

ASFA requires that a permanency hearing be held within 12 months after a child is considered to have entered foster care, every 12 months thereafter, and 30 days after a finding that reunification efforts are no longer required. At the hearing there must be a determination whether:

❖ the child should be returned to the parent;

❖ the child should be placed for adoption with the state filing a petition for termination of parental rights;

❖ the child should be placed with a fit and willing relative;

❖ the child should be referred for legal guardianship; or

❖ the child should be placed in another planned permanent living arrangement where compelling reasons exist.

For children 16 or over, the hearing is to determine what services are needed to assist the child in making the transition from foster care to independent living. 42 U.S.C. § 675(5)(C). Further, if the child is in an out-of-state placement, the court is to determine whether the placement continues to be appropriate and in the child's best interests.

The permanency hearing was intended by Congress to be the hearing at which a definitive permanent plan would be set for each child. Previously, such hearings were only required at the 18-month mark and, in reality, all that was needed was a court order authorizing continued placement for a specified period.

Many agencies have had difficulty complying with the permanency hearing requirement because court hearings sometimes are delayed. Unless state law sets the deadline based on the date of the child's removal, the 12-month deadline for the permanency hearing begins to run from the time that the child is "considered to have entered foster care." That date is either the date the court found that the child was abused or neglected or 60 days after the child's removal from home, whichever comes first.

It is important to explain to the courts the nuances of this deadline and that the hearing must take place within 12 months after a child is considered to have entered foster care. It is often helpful to bring a copy of the statute (or an excerpt) to show to judges. It is also helpful to explain the deadline in terms of the stages of the court process in the local community.

One good way to minimize the problem of delays is to establish policy requiring the agency to request the permanency hearing far in advance of the 12-month deadline. An even more helpful approach is to propose changes in state law requiring the hearing one year after placement or even earlier. A deadline calculated from the date of placement is simpler for all concerned.

Technically, it is not necessary that the court itself conduct the permanency hearing. Instead, the hearing can be conducted by an "administrative body appointed or approved by the court." 42 U.S.C. § 675(5) (C).

Realistically, however, few agencies are able to conduct hearings themselves, even if the court approves. The term *hearing*, in this case, means that due process protections are required. The only way for agencies properly to conduct permanency hearings themselves is to use legally trained administrative hearing officers (with court approval). Unless administrative hearing officers are already heavily involved in child welfare cases, the best approach is to have the court conduct the permanency hearing.

For compliance purposes, the permanency hearing is different from the six-month review in one critical respect. While the six-month review must address several issues, the permanency hearing is to result in a permanent decision. That is, while the purpose of the six-month review is to review case progress (analyzing several specific issues), the permanency hearing is supposed to choose from among permanent legal options for the child. And, significantly, there is no option to continue open-ended stays in foster care.

Thus, compliance with the two requirements is different: for the six-month review, specific issues must be addressed, but at the permanency hearing the court must take the action of returning the child home, freeing the child for adoption, etc.

The permanency hearings required by ASFA provide an opportunity to ensure a permanent home for abused and neglected children. It is intended to be an in-depth, systematic look at the options provided under the statute.

Cooperation between the agency and the court is essential to the success of the permanency hearing and determining a permanency plan for the child. Detailed checklists, sample court reports, and sample court orders to guide the process can be found in C. Fiermonte and J. Renne, *Making It Permanent* (ABA 2002).

Strategies Regarding Reviews of Voluntary Placements

Federal law allows states to collect federal matching funds for certain children in voluntary (not court-ordered) foster care for up to 180 days after placement. However, to be eligible for federal reimbursement beyond the 180 days, there must have been a judicial determination, before the 180 days expired, "to the effect that such placement is in the best interests of the child." 42 U.S.C. § 672(e).

Many states do not use voluntary placements, except in uncommon circumstances, and, even then, for only short periods of time. In such states, within a short time after the occasional voluntary placement, either the child will be returned home or a juvenile court proceeding will be initiated. In these states, compliance with 42 U.S.C. § 672(e) presents no difficulty.

States with a history of many voluntary foster placements have taken a number of approaches to achieve compliance. Some have simply shortened the time periods that they will allow non court-approved foster placements.

A few states use a special process to obtain court approval of voluntary placements. This process is different from the usual court process for child abuse and neglect cases, in that court approval of voluntary placements does not require allegations of abuse and neglect. In addition, while permanency hearings are still required, the supervisory role of the court may be limited.

Important Issues for Court and Agency Collaboration

In at least one state, due process protections to parents are minimal in court proceedings to approve voluntary placements.

One approach is to establish a special court procedure exclusively for the voluntary placement of certain special needs children. The procedure would apply only to children who are to enter state supervised group or institutional care because of their own special needs rather than because of parental abuse or neglect.

The special procedure would allow the court to approve the placement of such children into foster care based on the children's special needs without a finding of abuse or neglect and without a loss of parental custody. The procedure would be allowed only in cases in which there has been no abuse or neglect.

The reason for enacting a law establishing such a procedure is simple: avoiding needless state interference with the independence of families. In cases involving the foster placement of handicapped children, where there are no real allegations of child maltreatment, a juvenile court process with allegations of parental fault is inappropriate and the loss of parental custody is unnecessary.

By adopting such a procedure, it should be possible to obtain federal matching funds for the cost of foster care. Nothing in federal law requires a finding of abuse or neglect to be eligible for matching funds; what is required is a finding that foster care was necessary because continued placement in the home would be contrary to the welfare of the child. 42 U.S.C. § 672(a)(1).

Transfer of parental custody is unnecessary because federal law requires the agency to be "responsible for the child's placement and care" rather than necessarily to have custody of the child. 42 U.S.C. § 672(a)(2). So long as the agency plays an *active* oversight role, this requirement should be fulfilled.

However, such an approach should also include specific protections to prevent children from being easily allowed to enter care and then being "warehoused" in care. To protect against children from being placed inappropriately or left needlessly long in group and institutional facilities, the following are some needed protections:

- ❖ strict agency policy forbidding the use of the special court procedures described above when children are believed to have been maltreated;

- ❖ an internal agency screening process to assure that the special court procedure will not be used when children are believed to have been maltreated;

- ❖ specific requirements concerning opportunities for parents to remain involved with their children after placement into group and institutional care;

- ❖ notice to parents concerning their obligation to remain involved and the legal risks if they do not remain involved;

- ❖ case plans, periodic reviews, and other protections required by federal law;

- ❖ mandatory child neglect reporting by group and institutional care facilities when parents cease regular contacts with their children after placement;

- ❖ agency intervention on behalf of children in group and institutional care facilities after learning that parents have ceased to be involved; and

- ❖ permanent placements for those children who have been abandoned in group and institutional care facilities and who are capable of functioning in family settings.

Delinquency and Status Offenses

Agencies may collect foster care matching funds for certain delinquents and status offenders in foster care placements as long as the facilities are not "detention facilities, forestry camps, training schools, or any other facility operated primarily for the detention of children who are determined to be delinquent." 42 U.S.C. § 672(a)(3), (c)(2). However, as explained in the above discussion of the judicial determination requirements, there are some special challenges in obtaining appropriate court orders for such children.

To claim federal matching funds, the state must comply with ASFA's requirements. Certain ASFA provisions apply when the child is *first removed* from the home, such as *contrary to the welfare* and *reasonable efforts* determinations.

Other ASFA requirements apply after eligibility for foster care is established, such as periodic reviews and permanency hearings. For a detailed discussion of the application of ASFA to delinquency and status offense placements, see Chapter 21 in D. Ratterman Baker, *et al., Making Sense of the ASFA Regulations: A Roadmap for Effective Implementation* (ABA 2001).

As a practical matter, reasonable efforts on behalf of delinquent children and their families may be much different from those for dependent children. For example, the agency might need to focus on preventing deterioration of the child's behavior or establish means for restitution to be made.

Efforts to prevent removal may be impractical because the arrest situation prevents any efforts at all or the state has no knowledge of the family. In that case, because nothing else could have been done, the lack of efforts may be considered "reasonable."

In many states, the courts themselves operate foster and group facilities for status offenders and children found to have been delinquent. If the agency and courts are willing to enter into contractual arrangements, the state can be eligible for federal matching funds for such children.
42 U.S.C. § 672(a)(2)(B).

However, to avoid the risk of sanctions against the state as the result of federal reviews, all federal foster care requirements must be met for such children, such as periodic reviews, permanency hearings, and written case plans meeting all federal specifications.

Receipt of federal matching funds can help the courts provide better foster care for juvenile justice youth. The funds may help them upgrade their placements and services. Struggling to meet the federal requirements may cause them to update their programs. Accordingly, if it appears administratively feasible and courts have demonstrated their willingness and ability to comply with federal requirements, it is a good idea to allow courts to receive federal matching funds for their own foster care programs.

Agencies should be prepared to provide technical assistance to courts' administrative staff in order to help them comply. Such assistance might include, for example, instruction of the development of case plans for status offenders and delinquents. Technical assistance should also include help with the development of forms.

On the other hand, agencies need to protect themselves against the financial brunt of negative federal reviews, should the courts' administrative staff fail to comply with federal requirements. Therefore, agencies should negotiate strict agreements before allowing courts to receive federal matching funds for their foster care programs.

Courts should be required to agree to financial penalties for noncompliance with federal requirements, particularly when court noncompliance causes the state to fail a federal review. The agreement should also allow the state agency to monitor court compliance.

Finally, note that some courts choose not to try to receive federal matching funds because it is beyond their capacity to comply with federal requirements. Compliance may be difficult because of the size of a rural court's foster care program. Or, compliance may be difficult because existing weaknesses in the court's services to children would make compliance very expensive. For example, if a court currently uses probation officers with caseloads of 150 as case managers, it would have to hire many more probation officers to be able to prepare individualized case plans in compliance with federal law.

Caseworker Waiting Time

A major issue for many agencies is that their caseworkers spend a great deal of their time in court waiting for hearings to begin. The complaint is not necessarily that caseworkers have to go to a large number of hearings or that they must spend a great deal of time preparing for court. Rather, the problem is that every time caseworkers go to court, they spend long periods of idle time waiting for hearings.

While some waiting time is unavoidable and while hearings cannot always proceed precisely on schedule, some courts are able to operate with far less waiting time than others. In some courts, caseworkers routinely must wait hours before participating in a single hearing lasting only a few minutes. In other courts, a waiting time of 20 minutes is normal. In still other courts, review hearings are clustered so that a single caseworker can have several routine review hearings heard in a row.

As a rough rule of thumb, if caseworkers have to wait for routine hearings an average of more than 45 minutes, the agency should regard this as a serious problem. This time period is an average only, and it is important to realize that there are many times when longer delays are unavoidable. But if it is typical for caseworkers to wait for hours before their hearings, it is reasonable to conclude that the practice is not fair to agencies, families, or children.

Of course, court waiting time is not something under the control of an agency administrator. The most an administrator can do is to document the problem and suggest solutions. Many judges are willing to listen to the agency and to entertain suggestions for improvement. However, this effort requires great tact on the part of the administrator and an understanding of the problems faced by the judiciary.

Long waiting periods are usually exacerbated by the court's large caseload. If that is the case, there may be something you can do to help a local court point out the problem to statewide court administrators or to the legislature. Working with the courts for this purpose is explained later in this book.

You may need to precisely document your waiting time in order to convince the key juvenile court judge or the administrative judge in charge of your local court system that agency waiting time is a significant problem. If documentation is necessary, consider the following approach.

- ❖ **First, ask caseworkers to record their in-court waiting time for a specific time period (such as a week).** For cases which were rescheduled due to a full docket and took place during the test week, also ask caseworkers to note their travel time and any projected extra time in preparing for the hearing when it comes back to court.

- ❖ **Second, after receiving this information, tabulate the total amount of waiting time.** To focus exclusively on *excessive* waiting time, subtract any waiting periods of less than one hour for hearings that were not rescheduled. For the cases continued due to a full docket, include the entire waiting period, plus travel time and any extra preparation that the caseworker was required to make as a result of the hearing being canceled.

❖ **Third, having calculated the total weekly hours of undue caseworker time in court hearings, calculate the total cost.** To make this calculation, do not include only the cost of caseworkers' salaries and benefits per hour, but rather use a loaded rate. The loaded rate should build in such costs as rent, administrative costs, etc. If the cost to the agency is great, that should make an impression on the court. Assuming that the caseworkers are spending a great deal of time in court, and assuming that you are very tactful, this cost figure should help the courts understand the gravity of the issue for the agency. Of course, if your court also hears other types of cases you also must understand that there are also costs involved in making others wait.

The following example illustrates how to calculate excess caseworker court time and how to compute its cost:

> Worker A went to court three times last week. Mr. A waited two hours for the first hearing to begin, one hour for the second, and one hour before learning that the third hearing was reset due to a crowded court docket. It took one hour in travel time to attend the third hearing, and the worker estimates that it will take an extra hour to prepare for the rescheduled hearing, including arranging for the parent to attend, rereading the case file, and other steps.
>
> Based on the above information, we can calculate that Mr. A spent four hours of excess court time during the week. This includes the extra hour of waiting for the first hearing, the hour traveling to the hearing that was reset, the hour waiting for the hearing that was reset, and the hour of projected extra preparation for the reset hearing. Thus, excess court time occupied 10% of Worker A's 40-hour work week.
>
> As it turns out, the average excess waiting time for all of the ten caseworkers for the local office averaged out to 10%. The state pays an average salary of $47,000 per year for the 10 workers, taking into account fringe benefits, unemployment tax, and social security and

Medicare taxes. Because there are 10 workers with an average salary of $47,000, 10% of their total salaries also equals $47,000.

Since the ultimate work product of the local branch of the child welfare agency is casework, a 10% pro rata share of all other expenses of the local office are factored in calculating the cost of excess court time. Clerical expenses, administrative salaries, rent, utilities, supplies, and other costs attributable to child welfare cases equals $190,000. Ten percent equals $19,000.

Therefore, if one projects the excess waiting time experienced during the sample week to occur throughout the year, the total annual cost to the local branch state child welfare agency from excess court waiting time is $47,000 + $19,000, or $68,000 per year.

Considering the documented costs in the above example, it is reasonable to ask the court to make adjustments. If administrative or procedural adjustments by the court or a small amount of added judicial time can sharply reduce excess worker waiting time and curtail the cancellation of hearings, such improvements are eminently logical.

To solve the problem of excessive waiting time, the most important thing that a court can do is to change the way that it dockets the hearings. The ideal approach is to set each hearing for a specific time (a *time certain*) and then generally to stick to those times. In the Hamilton County Juvenile Court in Cincinnati, Ohio, the court sets every hearing for a specific time, even shelter care and review hearings.

Hearings typically take place within 20 minutes of their scheduled time. However, that court has relatively low judicial caseloads and holds longer hearings than many other courts. Still, part of the reason for the uncrowded docket is that the court efficiently uses its time, grants few continuances, and spends little time sitting idle between hearings.

If a court cannot set all hearings for a time certain, the next best thing is to at least carve out a smaller block of time within which the agency hearings will take place. For example, some courts will schedule routine agency reviews the first thing in the morning or afternoon. If there are only a few reviews, agency staff will have to wait a short time.

Important Issues for Court and Agency Collaboration

Other courts might be willing to set aside some other specific time. For example, the court might set aside a specific hour and a half for several agency review hearings — 9:30 A.M. to 11:00 A.M. During this hour and a half, the agency review hearings will occur in a specific order.

The specified order will allow workers whose cases appear last on the list to show up one half-hour late. Those caseworkers whose cases are at the beginning of the list will be able to leave early.

It may even be possible to schedule hearings so that caseworkers can have several cases heard in a row. If attorney time is flexible, if caseworkers bring their calendars, and if court staff can set the next hearing when the parties are present in court, workers can ask for times when they are already coming to court.

Docketing systems vary, and each requires a unique solution. Consider the following example:

> In a rural judicial district, Judge S begins the morning by hearing uncontested motions which, altogether, usually take anywhere from five to 30 minutes. Next are contested motions, which, all together, usually take from 30 minutes to two hours, and finally there are review hearings. The caseworkers must show up and sit through the uncontested and contested motions.
>
> Because caseworkers were located only five minutes away from the courthouse, the following solution was worked out: Judge S agreed to continue holding the uncontested motions first, but once they are finished, to call the agency. After the telephone call, the judge would hear the first contested motion before the worker arrives.
>
> Upon the workers' arrival, the judge would hear review hearings. After the time set aside for review hearings, the judge would hear the remainder of the contested motions. Note that, except for the first one, the contested motions would be *set in advance* to follow the review hearings.

Another important step that can ease the impact of waiting time at court is to set aside special offices for caseworkers in the courthouse and to provide them with access to telephones. The child welfare agency should make known to the court its need for special rooms for caseworkers, for families and children, and for attorneys to meet with their clients. It is especially important to do this whenever the agency becomes aware that the juvenile court is being relocated.

Convenience of Expert Witnesses — Witness Waiting Time

Some agencies have difficulty convincing expert consultants such as physicians and psychologists to testify in court proceedings. Many experts do not want to testify because of prior experience spending a great deal of uncompensated time waiting to testify in court. Expert witnesses resent losing hours of work time sitting and waiting to testify and they resent the disruption of their practice.

When doctors and outside mental health professionals are called to testify, they may have to wait to testify not only because of slippage in the court docket but also because of the length of the hearing. Since expert witnesses are usually called in to testify in contested, and therefore relatively lengthy, hearings, they often have to wait during much of the hearing or trial before they have the chance to testify.

There are several steps that can be taken to reduce the waiting time for expert witnesses:

❖ **The court hearing can be set for a specific time** (time certain).

❖ **The less the hearing is delayed, the less waiting time for the expert.**

❖ **Arrangements can be made in advance to allow the expert to testify at a specific time, out of the regular order of witnesses.**

For example, if the agency presents its case first, it may have the expert testify at the beginning of the hearing. If the agency's case comes later, and the judge is agreeable, the agency's attorney may arrange with the judge in advance to have the expert testify at a specific time.

The agency attorney may feel, however, that calling the expert out of order detracts from the logical flow of the evidence. The attorney may even feel the need to devote extra preparation time to maintain the flow of evidence. However, if calling the expert out of order reduces the cost to the agency and ensures that a key expert will be available in the future, the arrangement is probably well worth the trouble.

- **The expert can be on call during the morning or afternoon in question and be notified shortly before being asked to testify.**

    When the agency is about ready to call the expert witness, the witness is contacted by telephone and asked to come into court. When the witness arrives, other testimony is interrupted until the expert is allowed to testify and then leave. These sorts of arrangements are especially common with physicians.

- **Electronic pagers can be used to contact the experts.**

    The pager may be an expert witness' regular pager or one furnished by the agency. Use of a pager allows the expert to be out of the office and working until the call is received.

- **Arrangements may be made for the expert to testify by telephone.**

    Where the attorneys agree, it may be possible to arrange for expert witnesses to testify by telephone. If testimony by telephone is permitted under state rules of procedure and the judge can be persuaded to go along with the arrangement, it can be helpful to both sides. If testimony is to be given by telephone, it is more convenient to the expert and it therefore should be easier to persuade the expert to testify. In addition, avoiding the expert's trip to court reduces the cost of the testimony to the agency or the court.

    Of course, a speaker phone is needed to allow for examination and cross-examination of expert witnesses in court. Testimony by telephone of expert witnesses is often used in child abuse and neglect cases in many courts. Generally, it requires a series of meetings to establish the practice of expert testimony by telephone.

    Note that while the court may be willing to allow expert testimony by telephone, it is less likely that this method will be permitted for the testimony of others. The judge needs to observe other witnesses to evaluate whether they are truthful. The truthfulness of expert witnesses such as mental health professionals is seldom at issue.

Making Sure That Experts Are Well Prepared to Testify

Another reason why some experts are reluctant to testify is their fear of embarrassment or frustration in court. While the agency cannot prevent a rigorous cross-examination, there are steps that can help the expert withstand the cross-examination.

The agency can make sure that the expert understands exactly the issues upon which the expert is to testify. The agency attorney should explain the issues in writing or, if that is not possible, the caseworker should do so, with a copy to the attorney.

The agency should also insist that its attorney offer to spend time with the expert witness to go over the witness' testimony at least two days before the hearing. This preparation allows the expert to make any further tests, to review the records, or to review the literature before trial.

Access to Court

In some places, agencies are unable to get adequate and timely access to the courts. Some agencies have to wait months to get on the court docket for the trial of an abuse or neglect case. When some agencies wish to change court orders concerning placement, visitation, or services, it takes months to accomplish.

Such problems can occur for several reasons. In a specialized juvenile court, there may not be enough judges. In a court that also hears other types of cases, the court may be overwhelmed by its entire caseload. Another possibility is that there is a presiding judge who is not aware of the agency's problems and has not set aside enough judicial time to hear child maltreatment cases.

Another reason may be that contested cases — which take far more time than uncontested ones — are not expected nor is time provided for them. Finally, part of the problem may be that the court is not well organized and there is a good deal of time when judges are not hearing cases, i.e., there is too much "judicial downtime."

If an agency, with the help of its attorney, can determine the cause of its lack of access to the courts, there may be steps that can be taken to address the problem. Just as with problems of caseworker waiting time, the agency needs to document the scope of the problem and the impact on its clients.

For example, an agency might document court delays in termination of parental rights proceedings and calculate the costs in terms of unnecessarily lengthy foster care. Of course, this type of communication needs to be very tactful. When raising such issues, it is wise to assume that the agency itself also contributes to the delays and to ask what the agency might do differently to alleviate the problems.

The agency should also be prepared to document the human costs of delays and lack of access to the courts. The agency should identify specific recent but now closed cases where progress was put on hold while waiting for the court to decide.

The agency should describe the experiences of caseworkers and clients while these delays occurred. The following is an example of a written anecdote that an agency might prepare:

> Last March, the Department and Mrs. S.W. disagreed about whether Mrs. S.W. should submit to drug and psychiatric testing. On March 15, the Department filed a motion to ask that the court order Mrs. S.W. to submit to the tests. The case came up for hearing on May 20, but Mrs. S.W. didn't appear. Judge O. reset the hearing for July 10.
>
> On July 10, the hearing had to be reset until September 5, because the court had allocated 20 minutes to the hearing and the attorneys' arguments were not completed in that time. At the September 5 hearing, nearly six months after the motion requesting an order to test was filed, the judge ordered Mrs. S.W. to take the tests.

By September 20, the tests were completed and the testers had prepared treatment recommendations for Mrs. S.W. She was then placed on a priority waiting list for treatment.

As the result of the delays in obtaining testing orders from the court, the initiation of treatment was delayed nearly six months. The agency was unable to complete its case plan, and the passage of time has made rehabilitation and reunification more difficult.

As a result, the child is likely to spend at least an extra six months in foster care, at a cost of approximately $—, including foster payments and apportioned administrative costs for one child in care. In addition, it will be very difficult for this case to comply with federal timelines.

When faced with such problems in individual cases, the agency and its attorney must do their best to press for the earliest possible hearing and jockey for adequate court time. The agency needs to set strict internal policy to make sure that *it* is not requesting unnecessary delays. Its attorney should oppose needless requests for delays by other attorneys and should provide them with information promptly so that they do not have legitimate excuses for delays.

When requesting early hearings and adequate docket time, the agency should remember to remind the judge of the human cost in the individual case. For example, if there have been related delays in the trial, let the judge know how stressful delays are on the child and, perhaps, what the child's psychiatrist has said about such stress. For example, let the judge know that a treatment facility has an opening now and that if the treatment order is delayed for over a month, space may no longer be available.

Another adverse effect of insufficient court time can be that the court, to free up time on the docket, may put pressure on the agency to settle cases inappropriately. For example, the court may press the agency to agree to less serious allegations against parents in order to secure an agreement for placement into foster care.

The judge might press an agency to agree to a finding that the parents are "in need of services" rather than that they physically abused the child. The problem is that if the parents later adamantly refuse to participate in treatment related to their physical abuse of the child, the agency may be in a weak position to compel them to participate or to terminate their rights for refusing.

Agencies must resist inappropriate settlements by explaining to the judge their reasons for doing so and by dramatizing their potential human cost. Unfortunately, however, when there is inadequate available court time, the agency may sometimes be faced with a difficult choice between an insufficient settlement and substantial delays.

As suggested later in this book, agencies facing these types of problems need to become involved in court reform efforts. Agencies need to document the overall impact of the problems on children, families, and their own operations. They need to try to forge alliances with judges in order to lend support to their reform efforts.

Getting Judges to Accept Child Witness Reforms

Over the past decade, many child welfare reforms have been developed to make the courtroom less traumatic to children. Many agencies need to ask courts to adopt appropriate child witness reforms. These reforms may include:

- allowing children to visit the courtroom early and talk to the judge;
- designing a less intimidating courtroom for children;
- having a playroom for children while waiting for court to begin;
- allowing small children to sit in a relative's lap while testifying;
- allowing the judge to interview children in chambers if attorneys consent;
- sometimes using videotaped testimony in lieu of court appearances (when personal testimony by the child is not practical and videotaped testimony does not violate due process); or

❖ using closed circuit television so the child does not have to face the alleged abuser in the same room.

The legal barriers to achieving such reforms are less in juvenile court child protection cases than in criminal proceedings, because certain provisions in the United States Constitution apply in criminal cases but not in juvenile court. In addition, while various constitutional rights applicable to criminal cases have been well defined through appellate decisions, juvenile court procedure must adhere to the less well-defined standard of *due process of law*.

Thus, the key practical obstacles to achieving such reforms in juvenile court are less often constitutional barriers than in criminal proceedings. Instead, the key barriers are most often:

❖ the need to convince the judge, and

❖ the cost of the reforms.

While it is helpful to talk to court officials and to share literature describing child witness reforms, the most persuasive approach may be to offer peer examples. If there is another court in your state that has already adopted the reforms that you desire, it may be especially helpful to figure out a way to bring the other court to the attention of the judge. You may just inform the judge yourself or think of some way to encourage direct communication among the judges.

Many judges are cautious about instituting changes, and it is reassuring to know that a specific reform has worked in other places, especially within the same state. It may also help if you can think of a way that your judge can carry out the reform *even better* than the other court.

Another approach to achieving child witness reforms is simply to make a request, through your attorney, in an individual case. In case the judge does not readily grant the request, the attorney should be prepared with experts and literature to back up the request. Articles by other judges are especially helpful.

The agency should be aware, however, that the law may give the individual judge the discretion whether or not to implement the types of reforms outlined above.

Finally, child witness reforms are a very good topic for judicial training. Agency involvement regarding judicial training is discussed in chapter 2, *General Strategies for Working with Courts*.

Limiting Excess Judicial Interference with Casework and Resource Allocation

Many agencies complain about judicial micromanagement of agency casework or, to put it another way, "casework from the bench." This micromanagement involves situations where the judge spells out details of the agency's plan for the family, such as services, placement, and visitation, and, in doing so, interferes with the agency's ability to do its job. As noted above, a judge's unilateral decision to place a child in a specific placement without considering the agency's arguments will result in a loss of federal matching funds.

Sometimes the reason for judicial micromanagement of agencies is that the judge feels that the agency has not performed well in the past. If the agency also has not tried to work with the court to correct the problems, a conscientious judge may feel compelled to become involved in the details of decision making.

Regardless of the reason for persistent judicial involvement in the details of casework, it can create difficulties for the agency. Typical agency complaints about judicial micromanagement are as follows:

- ❖ Judges are inconsistent (both individually or from one another).

- ❖ Judges interfere with the agency's ability to set service priorities (by ordering services, judges make it difficult for the agency to plan for services and to set criteria for their use).

❖ Judges bring about an irrational allocation of agency services (e.g., by compelling the agency to spend inordinate time and expenses on some families, judges deprive other families of needed help).

❖ Judges are sometimes naive as to the consequences of their orders to the agency (e.g., when ordering the agency to use one service provider, the judge may not be aware that another provider does a better job of serving families with the precise problems experienced by the client).

One obvious way to address these problems is to try to identify and correct any inappropriate agency practices causing the judicial micromanagement. However, correcting agency practices may not be sufficient to eliminate inappropriate judicial interference. There are several other possible approaches that administrators should consider.

❖ First, make sure that agency attorneys emphasize in court any problems arising from specific court orders. The agency should work with the attorney to develop a strategy concerning how to explain the drawbacks of certain types of orders. In many cases, just making the judge aware of specific problems will be enough.

If the judge made a decision which is harmful for the child or causes either unreasonable expense or inconvenience to the agency, the attorney may be able to convince the judge to change the order. The judge probably did not issue the order because of intractable hostility or bias against the agency.

Most judicial mistakes are due to a lack of understanding of the situation; if there has been a clear misjudgment, it is usually best to assume that the judge would have acted differently had he or she better understood the situation. If you assume this to be true, then you can try to think of a way to help the judge to understand the problem better.

Try to think of a very tactful and uncritical way to raise the issue with the judge and to explain your point of view. Perhaps you can return to court and raise the issue again (i.e., by filing a motion for reconsideration based on additional evidence). When in court, the attorney will say something like, "Your honor, there are circumstances that may not have been clear at the earlier hearing, and we wish to take this opportunity to provide additional information."

- ❖ Second, when requests for judicial reconsideration do not work, the agency may choose to appeal. (See the discussion of appeals from "casework from the bench" in chapter 2, *General Strategies for Working with Courts*.)

- ❖ Third, set up meetings with the court to discuss the effect of judicial micromanagement on the agency. During the meetings, agency staff can describe the impact of judicial decisions on agency casework, services, and funding. The discussion can either proceed on a non case-specific basis, or may include discussions of specific cases that have already been permanently closed.

    Of course, the meeting may or may not succeed. With careful planning and presentation, the meeting may make the judge aware of certain casework and resource restraints. On the other hand, the judge may feel that resource distribution issues are not the court's concern and that the judge's only legitimate concerns are protection and best interests of the child in the individual case.

- ❖ Finally, the agency might want to propose legislation to narrow judges' overall authority concerning placement and services. However, the agency should be aware that proposing such legislation may stimulate a political conflict with the juvenile judges and with their organization that may ultimately prove counterproductive. Agencies should be especially cautious about taking extreme positions about what should be the powers of the juvenile courts.

Improving the Agency's Success Rate in Court

The agency's rate of success in court is important. Although most juvenile court cases are successfully negotiated by the parties, there are significant numbers of contested cases. Moreover, if the agency is successful in most contested cases, it can negotiate from strength in other cases.

Naturally, caseworkers want to be successful in court when a case is contested. It can be frustrating and disturbing when the court makes a decision counter to a worker's recommendations. The worker may feel frustration because of the worker's time investment, the possible impact on the worker's relationship with the family, or the worker's sincere belief that the court is doing the wrong thing for the family.

Nevertheless, agencies must accept graciously the reality of sometimes losing in court. Agency administrators should exercise leadership by encouraging caseworkers not to overemphasize losses in individual cases, not to become bitter or resentful toward the court, and to resist the very human impulse to retaliate against parents for winning a victory over the workers and agency.

Indeed, winning every case is not necessarily a positive thing. While the agency may ascribe a nearly unblemished win-loss record to superb case preparation and excellent choices of which cases to bring to court, there may be other, more negative possible explanations.

Some agencies nearly always win in court because they are too cautious in bringing cases to court and there are many children who are going needlessly unprotected. Still other agencies nearly always win because the judge is overly inclined to rule in favor of the agency in close cases.

While an agency should not expect to win all of its cases in court, it should expect the following:

❖ The agency does win a substantial majority of its cases.

❖ The agency and court apply relatively consistent criteria in case decisions.

❖ The agency generally feels that judicial criteria for decisions are appropriate — in other words, it generally feels that its philosophy and that of the court are in sync.

If *any* of the above are not true, your agency may need to reexamine the quality and vigor of its case preparation and presentation. For example, even if the agency is winning nearly all of its termination of parental rights cases, if there are cases it is not bringing when it believes termination to be appropriate, there is a problem that needs to be clarified and addressed.

Of course, administrators must accept that some cases cannot be brought because of state statutes or case law from appellate courts. But if the agency is not bringing cases because of a history of losses before its local judge, it may be due to poor preparation or excessive caution in bringing appeals.

Assuming that the agency loses cases because it is not well prepared for court, there are several steps that the agency should consider:

❖ **Establish regular legal skills training for caseworkers.** Training should include an in-depth introductory course and regular short courses on advanced skills and new developments. Training is more fully discussed in chapter 2, *General Strategies for Working with Courts*.

❖ **Enhance written materials on case preparation.** There should be complete case preparation checklists for caseworkers as well as well-written, completed forms. Different versions should be available for different types of cases faced by the agency. It is especially important to have well-designed checklists, forms, and samples for termination of parental rights cases. As the result of the Court Improvement Project grant, many states have developed sample checklists and forms. Check with the state Court Improvement Project Director to see if your state has information that is helpful to you.

❖ **Prepare protocols for the preparation of cases for court.** Protocols should spell out the respective responsibilities of supervisors, caseworkers, paralegals (if any), and attorneys, and should set a schedule applying to both. These protocols should, among other things, specify responsibilities and set deadlines for the preparation of specific court papers, and specify responsibilities for the identification and preparation of witnesses.

❖ **Take strong steps to improve the quality of agency legal representation.** This issue is discussed in more detail in chapter 5, *Improving Agency Legal Representation*. More detailed information about this topic can be found in M. Laver, *Foundations for Success: Strengthening Your Agency Attorney Office* (ABA 1999).

Special Projects to Alleviate Delays in Achieving the Termination of Parental Rights

Termination of parental rights cases, on the average, are the most challenging and difficult court cases faced by child welfare agencies. They are often rigorously contested and lengthy. The burden of proof is strict and appeals are frequent.

Some agencies have developed efficient techniques for the handling of termination cases. As early as the mid 1970's, pilot projects demonstrated how and when agencies should legally free children for adoption.

ASFA requires the state to file a termination of parental rights petition when a child has spent 15 of the last 22 months in foster care, calculated from the child's entry into foster care. Yet, nearly 30 years after some of the pilot projects and more than five years after the passage of ASFA, needless delays in achieving the termination of parental rights have persisted in many parts of the country.

At present, there are many agencies where the average involuntary termination of parental rights case is not completed until years after the child's removal from home. Yet there are agencies in which the average involuntary termination of parental rights case is completed within 15 months after placement.

Given the impact on children of delays in deciding whether to terminate parental rights, no state should tolerate a situation where long delays in termination cases are the norm. Such delays not only are stressful, but also can rob children of their chances for permanent homes.

Delays are also unnecessary and costly, as the modest financial investments needed to reduce termination delays are quickly recouped when children begin to leave state supported foster care more quickly. Even in cases where special needs adoption subsidies will be provided, speedier decisions save substantial administrative costs associated with foster care.

Agencies can borrow techniques from successful recent projects that have reduced delays in termination of parental rights cases. The ABA Center on Children and the Law has worked on one such project in New York, the Termination Barriers Project, and recently started similar projects in Pennsylvania, Kentucky, and Wyoming.

The following is a very brief overview of some of the key elements of the New York project, which started in 1989. To reduce delays in termination of parental rights cases, the state selected target counties with particularly egregious delays.

In each county, local staff was hired to work on the project, together with an ABA attorney. In each county, the project created joint task forces to reduce delays. The task forces included representatives from the agency, the agency attorney, the court, and other key representatives from the community.

The project began its work in each county by conducting a careful diagnosis of existing delays in legally freeing children for adoption. This diagnosis included assembling statistics concerning overall delays and isolating specific delays of several types:

- ❖ agency-centered delays,
- ❖ attorney-centered delays,
- ❖ court-centered delays, and
- ❖ delays due to problems in the working relationships among agencies, attorneys, and courts.

To diagnose such delays, the project used such techniques as detailed flow charts, case file readings, and careful interviews.

Important Issues for Court and Agency Collaboration

Having developed a clear overview of the entire process, identified the precise sources of delay, and measured the overall speed of termination cases, the New York project then set about eliminating the causes of delay. Project staff, in cooperation with each task force, began refining the process for preparing, presenting, and trying cases.

These efforts included both streamlining the agencies' internal procedures and altering court procedures causing delays in termination cases. It also included developing protocols to assist agency staff and attorneys to work more efficiently together.

Project staff, working with the task force, found that much delay was due to legal misunderstandings that could be corrected through training efforts and educational materials. Other delays were due to deficiencies in staffing. Needed were specialized agency staff, agency attorneys, and more available court time.

As of 2004, the Termination Barriers Project in New York completed its work in 14 counties, and is currently working in seven other counties. To date, the average estimated reduction in time it took for a child to move from placement to being freed for adoption is 15 months, with an estimated total foster care costs savings of over $14 million.

More recently, states have started innovative projects to help reduce delays, often with the help of federal grant funds, such as the Court Improvement Project Grant or the Adoption Opportunities Grant. Many states have developed drug or treatment courts that feature a special docket for parties with substance abuse problems, and the agency and court work closely with substance abuse treatment providers.

These specialized dockets allow for earlier identification and treatment of substance abusers, more stringent monitoring, and greater accountability. Some states are using improved technology or partnering with other branches of the court to provide drug or paternity testing. For example, in Idaho, one county uses the onsite drug testing available for juvenile cases to test parents in abuse and neglect cases where substance abuse may be an issue.

By considering such special projects, courts and agencies can work together to reduce needless delays and ensure that children achieve permanency as quickly as possible.

Agency-Court Collaboration in CFSRs and PIPs

Over the past several years, a new aspect of agency-court collaboration has involved the Child and Family Services Review (CFSRs) and the development of Program Improvement Plans (PIPs). As of 2004, all states have undergone the initial CFSR, consisting of a statewide assessment and on-site review overseen by HHS. For a discussion of the CFSR process, see Chapter 22 of *Making Sense of the ASFA Regulations: A Roadmap for Effective Implementation* (ABA 2001).

The CFSR focuses not just on the work of the child welfare agency, but on the entire state's performance with abused and neglected children. Courts make important decisions regarding the safety, permanency, and well-being of these children.

The court's active involvement is critical to a complete CFSR and a successful PIP. Therefore, to achieve the best possible results, you should collaborate with the court. Collaboration will help identify important judicial and legal issues within the court's control and allow court improvement issues into the agency reform agenda outlined in the PIP.

If you did not collaborate with the court for your state's initial CFSR, you should do so as your state prepares for subsequent CFSRs. The CFSR sets the agency's reform agenda for the future. Courts can help shape this agenda. You can point out the kinds of improvements the court might add to the agency's agenda through the CFSR process, e.g., improved agency court reports and testimony or helping courts obtain better performance data.

Work to engage the best people in the collaborative process. Solicit advice on the right judges and court staff to include in the CFSR and PIP development. Consider involving different people in different parts of the process or creating a special CFSR legal-judicial subcommittee to assist with the CFSR and PIP.

For more ideas on how to engage your court, see M. Hardin, *How and Why to Involve the Courts in Your Child and Family Services Review (CFSR): Suggestions for Agency Administrators* (ABA 2002), http://www.abanet.org/child/rclji/cp_agency.pdf.

4

Understanding the Juvenile Courts

How can you expect to work effectively with juvenile courts unless you understand how they think and work?

To develop a good relationship with courts, administrators need to transcend traditional agency attitudes about courts. Superficial attitudes about courts that overemphasize the personalities of individual judges or the supposed character traits of judges in general obscure important issues that agencies need to understand.

Administrators need a deeper understanding and broader vision. Administrators need to learn more about judges' points of view toward agencies and child welfare cases and about judges' typical likes and dislikes. Administrators need to get beyond such hostile or confrontational goals as "keeping judges out of our business" and think more profoundly about the appropriate role of courts.

Administrators need to learn more about how courts are run and some of their typical problems. Administrators need to stay informed about the latest technologies, pilot programs, and reforms being used by juvenile courts.

What Judges Want from Agencies

To work effectively with courts, a key is to be aware of what judges want from the agency. Paying attention to the legitimate needs of the judge makes it easier to obtain appropriate results in court.

Of course, there are important differences in what individual courts or judges want. Some judges hold relatively frequent hearings and, during their hearings, make in-depth inquiries about case progress; these judges want detailed information from agencies about their cases. These judges want agencies to keep them informed about important case events, such as movement of children to new placements, without waiting for the next regularly scheduled hearing.

On the other hand, some judges are not interested in the details of case planning. Once they decide that a child will go into foster care, they prefer to turn the case almost entirely over to the agency. Sometimes such differences in the degree of judicial involvement in case management reflect differences in state law or practice.

However, there are also wide variations in the depth of judicial involvement within many states. Agencies need to be aware of different judges' preferred level of involvement in case planning and to take account of those differences.

Putting aside differences in judges' level of involvement in child welfare cases, however, there are basic similarities in what judges want from agencies. Mostly, judges want agencies to do those things that help make judges' jobs easier and help judges to do their jobs better.

What can the agency do to help judges do their jobs? Most importantly, agencies can provide the court with high-quality testimony and information upon which to base decisions. Judges want hard facts and not just impressions of what is happening.

While judges do rely on the agency for recommendations, they want verifiable facts to support the agency's recommendations. That is why brief police reports are sometimes more helpful than lengthy but vague social work diagnostic opinions and impressions of what is happening.

With regard to reports submitted to the courts, most judges want:

- ❖ reports that reflect a thorough investigation or study of the case;

- ❖ reports that are well organized;

- ❖ reports that are easily understood and clear;

- reports that are brief and to the point — i.e., that address the points that are critical from a *legal* perspective;

- written information that can help them to complete any required judicial forms; and

- reports that precisely state their sources of information — i.e., whether first-hand observation or information from others and, if so, from whom.

When caseworkers testify, judges want:

- testimony that is presented in an order that is easily understandable;

- testimony that is, from the judge's perspective, to the point, without a lot of extraneous information;

- workers that have complete and up-to-date factual information about the case;

- testimony that is strictly accurate and truthful, especially descriptions of parental behavior and descriptions of what the agency has done to help;

- testimony that does not omit important details that the judge should know;

- candid information about the availability of agency services and assistance;

- punctuality in court appearances; and

- respect for the judge, court staff, and attorneys.

Besides getting good information on cases, judges expect their orders to be followed and their recommendations to be taken into account. Judges are especially concerned about this issue when they have an ongoing responsibility for the case, i.e., the case will return to the same judge at a later time. If there is a problem in carrying out the instructions of the judge, most judges do not want the agency either to blindly follow the instructions or to disregard them. Rather, they want to be informed of the problem when it occurs.

Judges want good casework by the agency. Good casework makes judges more secure that their decisions are appropriate and just. Only when everything reasonably possible has been done to help a family, and parents still did not improve, do judges feel comfortable with decisions abrogating parental rights.

Judges want timely casework and services. Courts are charged with making permanency planning decisions within particular periods of time, such as 12 months from placement. To meet their own decision-making deadlines, judges depend upon the agency to follow up on its service plan and to have services in place when they are needed. For the judge to carry out the intent of the law, speediness on the part of the agency is essential.

If caseworkers in your agency complain that they get a lack of respect from the judges, you need to find out whether the judges' attitudes are partly due to poor agency performance. If the judges' jobs are made more difficult because of mediocre agency reports, testimony, compliance with judicial instructions, or casework, you can't solve the problem simply by talking to the judge.

In fact, judges may not tell you that they are frustrated with agency performance in court. They may not want to appear overly critical. They may be fatalistic about agency performance, just as many agency administrators are fatalistic about courts. Ask the judge what your agency could do better to help judges do their jobs. Make certain they understand that you really want to know.

Judges' Pet Peeves and What You Can Do About Them

Just as there are things that judges affirmatively want from agencies, there are things that agencies do that annoy many judges. Some things that are upsetting to judges may not be within your power to deal with, such as the fact that caseworkers do not always have enough time to do everything they should. However, many judicial complaints are legitimate and deserve administrative attention. This section identifies typical sources of judicial irritation that are justified and suggests ways for administrators to deal with them.

Complaints About Casework

Judges become particularly upset when caseworkers fail to follow through on case plans. It is very frustrating when little has happened since the last time the case was brought before the court — for example, when the worker failed to arrange for a key service or left clients to their own devices.

Help judges to understand caseload limitations, but encourage them to bring it to your attention if particular caseworkers seem to be repeatedly failing to follow through with their cases. If the judge feels that staff casework or follow-up is unusually poor in an individual case, encourage the judge to put the concern in writing and to make sure that you get a copy. Let the judge know that you will be sure to follow up.

When you learn of the judge's concerns in an individual case, consider appearing in court personally to try to work out the problem. If you appear on your own initiative and take a constructive approach, it is likely to make a positive impression on the judge.

Judges are sometimes concerned about the quality of case plans. They feel that caseworkers are using standardized "boilerplate" case plans rather than crafting individualized strategies suitable for the individual family. They feel that many workers are not aware of services in the community.

The best thing that the administrator can do is to listen to the judges' concerns, ask for examples, and make any necessary adjustments in training, educational materials, quality control, and internal case review. Again, let judges know what you are doing to respond to their concerns.

Complaints About Implementation of Judicial Orders or Recommendations

Even more frustrating to a juvenile court judge than a caseworker who has failed to follow through on an agency-generated plan is one who has failed to take specific steps ordered or recommended by the judge. For example, it is upsetting for a judge to discover at a review hearing that the judge's order, issued six months before, calling for an interstate home study and the referral of a client for drug treatment essentially has been ignored.

The administrator should make it known that caseworkers are expected to implement court orders strictly and, if there are any problems in doing so, they are expected to bring such problems to the attention of supervisors. If an agency believes an order to be illegal, it can be appealed; otherwise it must be obeyed.

It should also be agency policy that caseworkers will follow judicial recommendations unless the supervisor or branch manager instructs otherwise. If the worker is not to follow the recommendation, the supervisor should promptly let the judge know of the reasons for the agency's decision.

Judges have the power to fine or temporarily jail caseworkers for willful contempt of lawful orders. Nearly all judges are highly reluctant to do so except in the most extreme cases. You should encourage judges to bring examples of noncompliance to your attention, and then you should take action to correct the problem and let the judge know what has been done.

Complaints About the Agency's Case Preparation

Another frequent complaint of judges is that the agency brings poorly documented cases to court. This situation presents judges with an uncomfortable dilemma. Judges are permitted to base their rulings only upon evidence formally and properly presented to the court.

Where the evidence is insufficient and appears to be poorly prepared, judges sometimes feel forced to rule against the agency, even though they suspect that what the agency is requesting is best for the child. Judges also sometimes feel compelled to make a legally insupportable decision to remove a child, to adjust for the agency's poor case preparation.

To identify problems with your case preparation, try to meet with the judge to discuss closed cases that you have lost. Bring your attorney along. This meeting should give you some insight into flaws in agency case preparation and presentation — as seen by the judge. Also ask for general comments and complaints from the judge concerning your agency's case preparation.

Besides soliciting comments, try to involve your judge in talking to caseworkers. Let the judge explain to workers and agency attorneys what kinds of case documentation and testimony are convincing in abuse, neglect, and termination of parental rights cases.

At the same time, you need to concentrate on improving the quality of your legal representation. Legal skills training for caseworkers may be needed. Changes in legal representation and paralegal assistance for your workers and attorneys may be necessary. These changes are discussed elsewhere in this book.

The Wrong Agency Employees Appear at Hearings

Judges depend mostly on the agency to let them know what is going on in a case. If a new caseworker appears in court who previously has not been actively involved in the case or if only a supervisor appears and the supervisor does not know what is currently going on, the judge will be justifiably exasperated. Without an agency employee present who knows the case, the judge cannot make an informed decision. The whole purpose of the hearing is undermined.

Certainly, caseworkers or supervisors who know the case should be present at court. At the same time, however, administrators must consider the burdens that court appearances place upon workers.

Administrators especially need to be conscious of problems, such as excessive waiting time in court and court scheduling that causes workers to appear for brief hearings on many separate days.

If part of the reason why the right caseworkers sometimes do not appear in court is that there are unreasonable waiting periods for routine hearings, try to work out a compromise with the court. Agree to firm policy concerning who must appear in court, but ask the court for assistance. Suggest that the court rearrange docketing to reduce waiting time in court and try to cluster hearings for individual workers to reduce the times that they must come to court.

After discussions with local agencies, one rural court adopted the following approach to ease waiting time for routine review hearings:

The court agreed to schedule its six-month review hearings during specific blocks of time to occur at the same time each month. Such scheduling would avoid requiring caseworkers to go back and forth to the court too often.

There were two agency branch offices in the particular judicial district. The court set aside the afternoon of the third Tuesday of each month for reviews held by branch office 1. The court set aside the afternoon of the second Tuesday for reviews for branch office 2. In addition, the court decided to allow caseworkers to schedule reviews a month or two early, if that would save them extra trips to court.

The agency promised to make sure that the caseworker or caseworkers most knowledgeable about each case would be present.

The issue of caseworker waiting time is discussed in greater detail in chapter 3, *Important Issues for Court and Agency Collaboration.*

Complaints About Agency Court Reports

When workers submit case reports just as a hearing is about to begin, they frustrate the decision-making process. This practice prevents the judge from reading the report in advance and thinking carefully about the case.

Last-minute submission of reports also denies attorneys and CASA volunteers the opportunity to review the report, investigate its assertions, and prepare questions to ask during the hearing. Judges are concerned that late submission of reports undermines the depth and quality of their hearings.

According to one judge:

> Time after time, we have workers who turn in their reports at the last minute. More than likely, the attorneys get the report just as the court hearing is about to begin and the attorneys have to spend time going over the report with the child and the parents during the time that the hearing was supposed to take place.

The next thing we know, an attorney wants to object to the worker's recommendations. That means that we have to schedule another hearing to hear evidence regarding the attorney's objection.

If the report had been sent to the attorneys earlier, I could require the attorneys to file their objections in advance. That would allow everything to be resolved at the original time set for the hearing.

To address concerns about untimely reports, administrators need to cooperate with the court in establishing and enforcing strict policies about when court reports are to be filed. Make sure, if possible, that judges are satisfied with the agency policy.

In addition, judges are sometimes concerned about the quality of court reports. They may feel that they receive incomplete or inaccurate information. They may feel that much of the information provided in reports is legally irrelevant and therefore does not help them to make decisions.

Even if they don't raise the issue, it is a good idea to ask judges for criticism concerning the quality of reports. Try to find out what the judges want from your reports, how they use the information, and how the reports might be changed to help them more.

Remember that the purpose of the reports is to persuade judges to make decisions that are in the best interests of children. If agency reports meet judges' needs, they will also be more influential. That is, if reports are modified in accordance with the needs of judges, judges will read the reports more carefully and rely on them more in reaching decisions.

Complaints About Agency Testimony

Judges are often dissatisfied with the testimony of caseworkers. The greatest cause of such dissatisfaction is the lack of good advance preparation. For example, it wastes court time when the caseworker does not have command of the facts of the case and continually must refer to the case file to answer questions. Even worse, of course, is when the worker doesn't know the facts and can't find them in the case file.

Another example of inadequate advance preparation is when agency attorneys and caseworkers do not discuss a case before coming to court. Since it is the attorney who asks questions and makes statements to the court, this lack of prior discussion can prevent important information from coming to the judge's attention.

Furthermore, it can slow down the proceedings when the worker has to whisper to the attorney or interrupt the proceedings. Equally disruptive is the situation where the various parties did not discuss the case before coming to court and are negotiating in the courtroom. Both kinds of behavior waste the judge's time.

Another cause of judicial frustration is the caseworker who is argumentative during testimony rather than strictly factual. For example, a worker may offer unsolicited opinions, give information not relevant to a question, or argue with the questioner. Such responses are distracting and make it harder for the judge to sift through the facts and figure out what is happening in the case.

Sometimes caseworkers testify in vague and pejorative generalities, such as by characterizing clients rather than precisely describing their behavior. For example, a worker may call a client "resistive," "manipulative," "punitive," or "defensive" without actually saying what the clients did to deserve that description. The worker may say that household conditions were "deplorable" rather than providing a precise description. It is difficult for the judge to determine whether the worker is overly judgmental or there really are severe problems.

Worst of all, judges sometimes get the sense that particular caseworkers are not accurate when testifying. On occasion, workers may confuse the facts, shade the truth, willfully leave out pertinent information, or even outright lie. For example, when pressed, some workers may be tempted to exaggerate or misstate their efforts to assist a client. Any appearance of a lack of candor or accuracy creates a risk that the entire testimony will be disregarded or given less weight as biased.

The important thing to do is to find out if these types of problems arise. Most judges will not take the initiative to tell you. Show up at court hearings unannounced from time to time. If you have confidence in your agency's attorney, ask about the quality of preparation and testimony from workers. Ask for specifics.

Talk to the attorney about the procedure used to prepare caseworkers for hearings. There should be at least a telephone contact between the worker and attorney before the day of trial for every hearing that the worker is expected to attend, no matter how routine. In contested cases, the advance meetings between worker and attorney should be face-to-face and extensive. If these things aren't happening, you cannot expect good results in court.

Recurrent problems in the quality of caseworker testimony suggest the need for training of workers, which is discussed in chapter 2, *General Strategies for Working with Courts*. It also suggests the possibility of substandard agency legal representation, which is discussed in chapter 5, *Improving Agency Legal Representation*.

Poor Preparation of Expert Witnesses

The examination and cross-examination of expert witnesses, such as physicians, psychiatrists, and psychologists can take up a great deal of court time. For the judge, such testimony is seen as wasting court time when the expert is not offering information which is useful to the court in reaching a conclusion. This situation most often occurs when the expert did not fully understand the purpose of the testimony before coming to court.

Both caseworkers and attorneys need to take the responsibility to prepare the expert for court. If an expert is to conduct an evaluation, the expert needs to be informed of the precise questions to be answered before the evaluation ever takes place. For example, if the question before the court is whether there is a reasonable possibility that the parent can improve enough within 12 months to allow the child's safe return home, that should be posed to the expert in writing before the examination.

Whether or not the expert conducted an evaluation at the request of the agency, the expert has the right to expect the attorney to spend time with the expert preparing the expert to testify. If this preparation is not consistently happening in your agency, expert witnesses will be less likely to want to testify and will be less effective in court.

Prior to the day of trial, the attorney needs to meet with the expert to explain the types of questions likely to be asked and the reasons for the questions. This meeting allows the expert time to review the case records, think about the questions, and possibly even to conduct a supplemental examination.

When such preparation is not done, the witness is more likely to appear ill-informed and unprepared. In addition, without preparation, the witness may actually come to court prepared to address the wrong issues. Unfortunately, this scenario is not unusual in many agencies.

Frequent Requests for Continuances

In many courts, hearings are frequently delayed or "continued" to another date. Hearings that are canceled at the last minute cause judges to be idle. When delays and rescheduling are common, it becomes very difficult for judges to schedule hearings for definite times.

This problem, in turn, increases worker waiting time. Moreover, rescheduled hearings force workers to make unneeded court appearances, delay justice for parents, and delay permanency for children.

Therefore, agency attorneys and staff should not often be the cause of delayed hearings. Rather, whenever possible, they should rigorously oppose such delays. It is true that, on occasion, a legitimate cause for delay will arise, such as that a key witness is ill. But absent such justification, caseworkers and attorneys should not delay hearings. Organizational problems within the agency, contributing to court delays, must be rigorously identified and eliminated.

Parents Are Not Present at the Hearing

To the judge, the parents' presence at a hearing is essential. Parents need to be present to provide critical information to the court and to be notified of their rights.

When parents are often not present at hearings, judges may assume that caseworkers are not doing enough to notify parents or are not actively encouraging them to attend. While the court has a responsibility to provide notice, it is the worker who ordinarily has the more frequent contacts with the parents. Accordingly, the workers' attitudes and statements to the parents often have great influence concerning whether they actually attend court hearings. Consider the following example:

> In one urban court, parents show up in the great majority of cases at the first court hearing, even in cases involving emergency foster care. Even non-custodial and unwed fathers who live in the area appear in most cases at the first hearing.
>
> In that court, caseworkers know that when parents do not appear at the first hearings, the workers will have to attend an extra hearing within a week to explain why parents are not present. In addition, the agency has cooperated with the court in making it clear to workers that they are to do everything possible to persuade parents to attend.

What You Can Do to Make Your Judges' Jobs Easier

What can you offer to make your judges' jobs easier? Reading over the preceding text with your local judges in mind, begin to compile a list. Ask your attorneys and staff to help. Then consult with your judge.

For example, in order to improve your relationship with the court, perhaps you will decide that your priorities are as follows:

- ❖ You will encourage the judge to share complaints with you and will respond to them quickly and effectively.

- ❖ Workers will prepare better documentation and reports.

- ❖ Workers will consistently get reports in on time.

- ❖ Workers will be prepared and knowledgeable about each case when going into court.

After setting these priorities, your next task will be to develop a detailed plan to make these things happen in cooperation your senior staff, your attorneys, and local judges. You will need feedback from your attorneys and judges as you proceed.

Serious Problems with Individual Judges

If you think that you have a problem judge, the first thing that you should do is to make sure whether the judge is really your problem. In reality, the judge, your legal representatives, and your caseworkers may all need to improve performance, and addressing the latter two issues may help. Or, perhaps you have a very active and assertive judge but your workers do not accept that it is the judge's job to be demanding, to protect parents' rights, and to expect strong evidence.

On the other hand, there are judges with whom agencies have an unusually difficult working relationship. There are judges who are arbitrary and unpredictable in their decisions. There are judges who are not interested in abuse and neglect cases and give them very low priority. There are judges who are unrelentingly hostile to the agency, the parents, or both.

Dealing with difficult judges requires the utmost tact, assertiveness, and determination. The sections that follow discuss specific problems with judges that may arise in child welfare cases.

Judge Bashing: What Not to Do

Like other people, judges are sensitive to criticism. Sometimes when agency personnel talk about judges among themselves or to others in the community, they forget that what they say may get back to the judge. When this happens, the working relationship between the agency and court can seriously be undermined, much to the detriment of families and children as well as the agency itself.

Besides damaging the agency's crucial relationship with the court, "judge bashing" has a subtle but corrosive impact on the culture within the agency. Judge bashing breeds cynicism, alienation, and defeatism. These are not attitudes that are conducive to good child welfare practice.

Sometimes judge bashing is the result of poor casework, case preparation, or testimony. In other words, hostility to the court may be a reaction to losing in court, which may in turn be the result of doing a poor job preparing and presenting cases. Administrators should not disregard "horror stories" about the court, but need to be aware of how the agency may have contributed to the result. Outrageous judicial decisions mostly occur in cases that are not well prepared and presented by the agency.

For all of these reasons, discourage caseworkers and supervisors from thoughtless criticism of the court. Help workers understand *why* the court behaves the way it does and to understand that the court performs a needed function, even if the agency sometimes disagrees in individual cases. Try to help workers and supervisors not to feel bitter when they occasionally lose a court case.

Agencies need to accept the basic nature of the court process. When it is not working as it should, caseworkers and administrators should feel empowered to take constructive steps to try to make improvements. The average judge is very eager to do a good job for abused and neglected children and will listen to well-considered complaints and suggestions, so long as they are not critical or insulting.

The Judge Who Blasts Caseworkers

In some cases, the stress of court hearings is exacerbated by hostile and disrespectful attitudes by judges. This problem may not be universal within a given court, but there may be one particularly harsh judge or certain caseworkers who seem to bear the brunt of judicial criticism.

To address these types of problems, meetings with judges are obviously required. The important thing is to come to the meetings properly prepared. If there have been any extreme incidents, the administrator should be prepared to discuss them specifically. If the situation reported was truly unusual or outrageous, it may make sense to request a transcript from the court hearing to verify whether it has been reported accurately. In rare cases involving highly abusive or insulting comments, it might even be appropriate to make a report to the state's judicial fitness committee.

Of course, it is not inappropriate for a judge to offer criticism in cases where workers have been negligent in their work on a case. It is counterproductive, however, for judges to be constantly frustrated and to ventilate their frustration on workers.

To avoid such problems, the best approach for the agency is to try to identify a more productive way for the judge to bring problems to the attention of the agency. The agency's willingness to recognize and correct problems experienced by the judge is probably the best way to alleviate this frustration.

For example, a judge may be harsh to caseworkers out of frustration that workers are not submitting reports on time and are coming to court unprepared. To change the judge's attitude, the agency may want to institute reforms to improve court preparation and to establish internal discipline concerning the timely filing of reports. Administrators may want to encourage the judge to keep the agency informed of its progress in correcting the problems and to identify any egregious lapses.

Agency attorneys should be expected to play a role in protecting caseworkers from embarrassment in court. The attorney should help workers prepare for court and speak up for them if they are subjected to unfair criticism.

The Judge Who "Shoots from the Hip"

Suppose that your juvenile court judge makes highly intuitive decisions or decisions based on his or her own personal knowledge of the community, instead of making decisions based strictly upon the evidence before the court. Consider the following situation:

> Agency caseworkers complain that a Judge X is unpredictable and inconsistent in his decisions. Workers and agency attorneys do not know what to expect regardless of the facts and their preparation in the case. Judge X has lived many years in the local community, feels he knows it better than most agency workers, and says that he bases his decisions on his knowledge and understanding of the community and its people.

To deal with judges like Judge X, the agency must take extra care in preparing its cases. If the judge makes an order with which the agency disagrees, it must explain immediately and precisely its problems with the order. If the agency was caught off guard in a hearing and was unable to explain why the judge's order is problematic, it should consider quickly asking the judge to reconsider the decision. To convince the judge to reconsider the decision, the agency will need to be very concrete and convincing.

As the agency administrator, you may need to remind the judge tactfully of the agency's potential loss of federal funds if a judge orders a placement without considering the agency's viewpoint. HHS has provided specific guidance on this point. Under Title IV-E, the child's placement and care must be vested with the agency. A court-ordered placement is prohibited when the court assumes "placement without bona fide consideration of the agency's recommendation regarding placement." *Questions and Answers on the Final Rule*, 65 FR 4020 (January 25, 2000), found in the *Child Welfare Policy Manual,* www.acf.hhs.gov/programs/cb/laws/cwpm/policy.jsp.

This rule does not mean, however, that the court must always agree with the agency's recommendation. Rather, if "the court hears the relevant testimony and works with all the parties, including the agency with placement and care responsibility, to make appropriate decisions," payment will be allowed under Title IV-E. 65 FR 4020 (January 25, 2000).

Ultimately, the use of appeal should be a key part of agency strategy in dealing with Judge X if careful case preparation and education are not successful. If requests for reconsideration are unsuccessful in a case where the judge issues an order not based on any evidence before the court, the agency should discuss the possibility of appeal with its attorney.

Appeals not only may succeed in individual cases, but also may make the judge more cautious about disregarding agency recommendations. Agency appeals are discussed in more detail in chapter 2, *General Strategies for Working with Courts.*

The Judge Who Persistently Refuses to Remove Endangered Children or Terminate Parental Rights

There are agencies that are seriously out of sync with their judges in their approach to protecting children. Such agencies feel paralyzed to protect children because they have been repeatedly unsuccessful in court. It may be, for example, that the judge will not remove children from their homes in certain types of situations despite the agency's view that such children are in grave danger. For example, it may be that the judge will rarely, if ever, terminate parental rights.

If you and your attorney believe the judge's position is not legally correct, then you must be prepared to file appeals. As discussed above, this involves preparing selected cases very carefully and first appealing especially strong cases.

The following example illustrates how one rural agency dealt with such a situation:

> Judge Z adamantly and repeatedly refused to approve the removal of abused children from their homes. The attorneys working for the agency not only refused to appeal but began to refuse to even bring such cases to court saying they could not win.
>
> The agency was contracting with private attorneys to represent it on a part-time basis. These attorneys also tried other cases before the judge in their private practice. They were unwilling to offend the judge by filing appeals.
>
> The agency found a simple solution. It decided to contract with two other attorneys whose private practice was outside the county. After the new attorneys began to rigorously present abuse cases, the judge began to authorize the removal of children. The judge recognized the risk of being reversed on appeal and appeals became unnecessary.

The Judge Who Is Not Interested

If you are in a court where individual judges control their own dockets and a judge gives abuse and neglect cases low priority, the best overall strategy is to try to enhance that judge's emotional connection with child abuse and neglect cases. Avoid harsh or critical language toward the judge. Recognize that the judge's docket is very crowded with other types of important cases.

To make the judge more emotionally aware of the abused children, appeal to the judge's conscience. During court proceedings, ask your caseworkers and attorneys to show the judge pictures of the children and even to bring the children in to court when it will not be harmful to them.

Ask workers and attorneys to explain to the judge in very concrete terms the traumas children are going through as the result of court delays. Present anecdotes, for example, of how the child behaved after the last hearing was set back. While offering such anecdotes, do not be critical of the judge, but simply make sure that the judge is aware of the gravity of the situation.

Again, take advantage of joint training opportunities to provide child development experts who can speak about the court experience "through the eyes of the child." Provide judges with concrete scientific evidence to support the impact of extended delays on the life of young children.

Once your agency and its attorneys have made headway in sensitizing the judge to the impact of delays and the lack of time on the calendar, you can begin to make concrete suggestions. For concrete examples, see the discussion in chapter 3, *Important Issues for Court and Agency Collaboration*, concerning improving access to the court.

Emphasize positive reinforcement. When the judge does the agency any favor, express your gratitude, preferably in writing. Try to make it pleasant and rewarding for the judge to work with you.

The Judge Who Does Not Appreciate the Need for Permanency

It is critical that judges understand children's need for permanent and legally secure homes. There are two ways to educate judges concerning the importance of achieving permanency:

- ❖ The first is literally to educate the judge through the presentation of individual cases. After hearing many cases in which carefully chosen experts testify as to the need for permanency in individual cases, most judges will absorb the concept even though they have never been formally educated in child development.

- ❖ The second way to educate judges is through formal judicial education. The topic of agency involvement in judicial education is discussed in chapter 2, *General Strategies for Working with Courts*. On the specific topic of the need for permanency for abused and neglected children, charismatic speakers with particularly impressive credentials are the key. These speakers should include both distinguished judges and prestigious mental health professionals.

The Judge Who Is Reluctant to Meet with You

Some judges feel that it is improper to meet with agency administrators and that doing so will compromise their judicial neutrality and independence. Judicial ethics do not prohibit such meetings so long as individual cases are not discussed and the subject matter of the meetings is related to the operations of the court or the agency's performance in the court. See American Bar Association, *Model Code of Judicial Conduct*, Canon 4(C)(1) (1990); American Bar Association, *Model Code of Judicial Conduct*, Section 5(G) (1972). Nevertheless, some judges feel that such meetings may inappropriately influence them or create the appearance of a pro-agency and anti-defense bias.

This attitude is far from universal, however. Most judges are willing to meet with agency representatives, subject to time constraints and their perception of the usefulness of the meetings. No bias is implied where the judges are also open to meeting with representatives of the parents' or children's bar.

If your judge is unwilling to hold meetings with representatives of the agency, he or she may be willing to attend if there is a wider group of participants. Additional persons invited to participate might include parents and children's attorneys and representatives of private agencies.

Indeed, even if the judge is willing to meet separately with agency representatives, wider groups are often appropriate. For example, parents' and children's attorneys may have helpful ideas and concerns about problems such as court delay.

If the juvenile court judge who hears the agency's cases is unwilling or unable to assist the agency with a problem, there may be a judge at a higher level of authority with whom the agency can meet. For example, if the issue the agency is concerned about is judicial scheduling, there may be a presiding judge who has some control over this issue.

Of course, this kind of step is very delicate, since the trial judge has a great deal of power that affects the agency. The agency needs to figure out a way to speak to the presiding judge that implies as little criticism as possible of the trial judge. For example, the agency representative could say to the trial judge, "We recognize that many scheduling difficulties may be beyond your control, and we hope that a meeting with the presiding judge will help us all."

Agencies should also be aware that judicial administration is more collegial than agency administration. There may be no single individual who can unilaterally resolve issues of calendaring or scheduling. The agency may need to talk to a number of judges with whom it does not ordinarily communicate. Perhaps the agency, when first contacting the trial judge, should indicate its intention to talk to other sectors of the judiciary at the same time.

Actual Judicial Misconduct: Abusive Conduct, Gross and Blatant Errors, and Corruption

When agencies are unhappy about something a judge has done, there are several possibilities. The agency may have to live with the problem; it may be able to work it out with the judge; it may be able to file an appeal; in exceptional situations, it may be able to disqualify the judge from hearing a case; and on rare occasions, the agency may be able successfully to complain to a judicial fitness commission.

In some states, parties can file an affidavit to disqualify a judge in an individual case, even without proof of the judge's prejudice, bias, or personal interest in the case. Sometimes parties take this action when a particular judge becomes extremely erratic, unpredictable, or abusive. Consider the following example that occurred many years ago, when the author was practicing law:

> A previously highly regarded judge gradually became known for erratic and unpredictable decisions. Private attorneys began to file "affidavits of prejudice" automatically disqualifying the judge from hearing their cases. This practice increased to the point that it became difficult to find enough private attorneys who were willing to hear the judge's cases.
>
> Eventually, but only after the public defender began to file regular "affidavits of prejudice," the state judicial fitness committee launched an investigation.
>
> It turned out that the judge was suffering from a brain tumor which caused episodes of irrational behavior, and the judge had twice in the past two years placed herself in a residential psychiatric facility for treatment. The judicial fitness committee disqualified the judge from further service on the bench.

On those rare occasions when judicial behavior reaches the level of serious misconduct, agencies need to be aware of the recourse available to them.

If judicial misconduct seems unusual and extreme, consult with your attorney concerning the possibility of some form of judicial discipline. In some states, investigations of judicial misconduct are relatively swift and vigorous.

What Is the *Proper* Relationship Between the Agency and the Court?

An important step toward improving the agency's working relationship with the court is thinking, in somewhat abstract terms, what the relationship should be like. One tension between agencies and courts is that they sometimes have unrealistic or inappropriate expectations of one another.

Agency administrators should try to establish a cordial relationship with the court. Agency and court administrators should work closely together on mutual concerns. There should be mutual dialogue and periodic cooperation on instruction and training.

On the other hand, agency employees at all levels should expect there always to be a certain tension between themselves and court personnel. The job of the court is to screen and oversee certain agency decisions and actions, and such oversight necessarily causes some discomfort. The court cannot and should not always do what the agency wants.

The challenge for administrators is to make sure that this tension accomplishes its intended purpose, to sharpen agency practice and to catch errors, without getting out of control and breeding bitterness or antagonism.

Hazard: Succumbing to Worker Complaints

It is very easy for administrators to speak only to subordinates and to get a distorted view of the agency's disagreements with the court. Workers and supervisors sometimes become enraged about losing cases or being treated disrespectfully in court.

The administrator needs to be aware that caseworkers often have a grossly exaggerated idea of the significance of a lost case and often do not understand why the agency lost. The administrator needs to keep matters in perspective and to help agency employees do so as well. It is essential to talk to others outside the agency and to get their perspectives about what happens in court.

It is useful, from time to time, to talk about what happens in court to guardians ad litem (including volunteers), attorneys for parents, foster parents, and judges, not simply to workers.

The Need for the Court — Facing Up to It

To avoid falling prey to knee jerk reactions or the natural prejudices of child welfare professionals, it is also important to think deeply about the role of the court.

Here are some things to think about. Should we abolish the juvenile court? What problems would we have if the court didn't exist? Given the need for the court, what are the necessary (as opposed to unnecessary) discomforts and inconveniences that the agency must face?

Here are some reasons why child abuse and neglect cases need to be brought to the juvenile court, besides the fact that this is required by law:

- ❖ **The court prevents agency oppression of clients and abuse of power.**

    Caseworkers' power over families is great. With unrestrained power, terrible abuses would occasionally occur. As in all other professions, there are some unprincipled and vindictive workers.

- ❖ **The court prevents errors in decisions concerning families.**

    Sometimes juvenile court hearings correct agency errors or misjudgments. Sometimes agency employees catch mistakes in the course of preparing for court. Sometimes caseworkers are more careful in the first place partly because they know that cases must eventually be brought before the court.

There are good and bad judges just as there are good and bad caseworkers. The court is a basic and necessary part of our American system of checks and balances in government.

❖ The court helps limit public hostility toward the agency.

When hearing about incidents in which child welfare agencies have removed children or left them in foster care, members of the public also hear that the agency was given permission to do so by the court. While agencies are subject to a great deal of sometimes unfair criticism, criticism would be worse without the involvement of the court.

The role of the court reinforces public perceptions that justice is done in child abuse cases. It helps to counter public perceptions that the agency intervenes inappropriately.

❖ The court alleviates parents' perceptions of oppression by the agency and deflects some resentment from the agency.

When children are removed from the home, parents' resentment of the agency is reduced due to the involvement of the court. Parents know that they have had the opportunity to dispute the agency's actions against them but that an objective authority ruled in favor of the agency. In addition, the judge may partially replace the agency as the focus of parental resentment.

❖ The court is needed to reinforce as well as to actually enforce agency decisions.

When the judge instructs parents, further coercion usually is not necessary. The official status of the judge and the atmosphere of the courtroom have an impact that the agency alone cannot. In most particulars, the court and agency have common expectations of the parent and the judge reinforces the agency's expectations.

What Is the Legitimate Oversight Role of the Court?

Even assuming that the juvenile court plays an important and necessary role in child maltreatment cases, disagreements remain about how deeply the judge should intrude in agency decisions. The basic issue is when should the judge be expected to defer to the discretion of the agency regarding issues such as when to intervene, where to place the child, and what services to provide.

Of course, agencies should not always win in court and judges should not always defer to agency judgment in decisions concerning placement, services, and permanency planning. For example, if agency actions are illegal, unconstitutional, or discriminatory, few would deny that the court should be empowered to order the agency to stop.

If an agency refuses to remove a child from an abusive situation, few would disempower the court from dealing with the situation.

Yet, there are significant disagreements concerning the exact boundaries of judicial power:

❖ Should the court be able to specify the foster home in which a child will be placed?

❖ Should the court be empowered to set terms of visitation or refine the case plan?

❖ Should the court be empowered to specify the service provider?

There are several possible approaches to these questions:

(1) The court should be empowered to make decisions specifying foster placements, visitation, and services whenever necessary to protect the best interests of the child.

(2) The court should not be empowered to make such decisions.

(3) The court should be able to substitute its judgment for the agency only when there is specific and compelling evidence that the agency is incorrect or unwise.

This book will not attempt to resolve this controversial issue but administrators should be aware that there are thoughtful arguments for each position. See, e.g., Judge Leonard P. Edwards, "The Juvenile Court and the Role of the Juvenile Court Judge," *Juvenile and Family Court Journal*, Vol. 43, No. 2, pp. 1-45 (1992) (advocating approach #1, above); Michael King and Judith Trowell, *Children's Welfare and the Law: The Limits of Legal Intervention* (Sage 1992) (advocating approach #2, above); Bruce A. Boyer, "Jurisdictional Conflicts Between Juvenile Courts and Child Welfare Agencies: The Uneasy Relationship Between Institutional Co-Parents," 54 Md.L.Rev. 377 (1995) (advocating approach #3, above).

Juvenile Court Reform Efforts

As discussed earlier, agencies sometimes can play an important role in helping to achieve reforms in the juvenile court. This section provides more detailed information on key judicial reform issues and how agencies can help.

Providing Constructive Information About the Courts

Of course, the child welfare agency does not have the power to actually change the court. However, as pointed out earlier, the agency may be able to raise the courts' awareness of problems and may have the opportunity to join juvenile court judges to support reform efforts.

The agency can perform two key functions in documenting the need for court improvement. First, the agency can document how the court problems affect children. For example, an agency might:

- ❖ estimate children's added time in foster care due to court delays;

- ❖ explain what it feels like for children to appear in an overwhelmed and overcrowded courtroom;

- ❖ describe the stress on children and parents while they wait months for court decisions; and

- ❖ describe how children feel when they face a new judge every time they come back to court on the same case.

Besides documenting the effect of the court's problems on children, the agency can explain how the court's problems affect its own operations.

For example, the agency can:

- ❖ explain the extra cost of keeping children in foster care due to court delays;

- ❖ describe the time that caseworkers spend sitting idly in court waiting for hearings; and

- ❖ explain how long it takes to get into court when a court order needs to be revised.

In gathering such information, however, it is most important for the agency to be sure that agency action (or inaction) has not contributed to the delay that it is attributing to the court.

The idea that agency administrators should support court reform efforts is controversial. Some administrators prefer to have juvenile courts that are not fully functional, and prefer juvenile courts capable of conducting only extremely brief hearings. If the courts had more resources, these administrators believe, judges would only interfere more with agency decisionmaking. According to this view, upgrading the juvenile court would not be a net benefit to children and families.

Increasingly, however, other administrators believe that the courts perform an essential function and they need to be able to perform it well. These agency administrators feel confident that they can successfully deal with well-run courts and, in most cases, prevent judges from overstepping their bounds. They feel that an effective court will ultimately be beneficial to families and children.

Administrators interested in providing information in support of court reform efforts have a special need to understand how the courts' operations affect their agency.

They need to grasp the juvenile courts' problems, and they need to understand what changes could help the juvenile courts function better. They need to have a vision of how a good court should operate.

Some Important Variables in How Courts Are Organized: Things That Child Welfare Administrators Should Know About Juvenile Courts

This section outlines some important concepts concerning the organization and operations of juvenile courts. Understanding them should give the administrator a more objective understanding of the local court.

A well-run juvenile court should apply "caseflow management" techniques in child welfare cases. "Caseflow management" refers to an important set of concepts and techniques used in judicial administration. These concepts and techniques help courts avoid delays and use their time more efficiently.

Among the key elements of judicial caseflow management are the following:

❖ setting strict time standards for cases to be completed (and for different stages of the cases);

❖ setting strict policies limiting the cancellation and delay of judicial hearings (limiting *set overs* and *continuances*);

❖ setting hearings for precise times;

❖ ensuring that cases stay on the judicial calendar (e.g., by setting the time of the next hearing at the end of each hearing); and

❖ measuring the average timeliness of hearings.

Leading judicial organizations endorse and teach the concepts of judicial caseflow management. Recently, special attention has been given to the specific application of these techniques in child abuse and neglect cases. Since its publication in 1995, the *Resource Guidelines: Improving Court*

Practice in Child Abuse & Neglect Cases has served as an important guide for courts in improving and refining the child welfare court process.

The *Resource Guidelines* details how to conduct various hearings in child abuse and neglect cases, outlines characteristics of the judicial process that transcend specific hearing types, and addresses a wide range of important procedural issues, such as notice, who should be present, advice of rights, key judicial findings, and issues to present at different hearings. Through the Court Improvement Project, states have supported a variety of activities to implement the *Resource Guidelines*, including benchbooks, judicial checklists, and forms.

Another issue that is especially important to juvenile and family courts is the type of calendaring system used by the court. A key distinction is whether the court uses *master calendars*, *individual calendars*, or something in between.

In a court with a *master calendar*, as a case proceeds, each hearing can be assigned to a different judge than the judge who conducted the last hearing. For example, in one court with a master calendar, different judges are assigned to handle child abuse and neglect cases on different days. Whoever draws a particular day presides over all of the hearings set for that day. Usually, there will be a different judge than the one who presided over the last hearing.

In large juvenile courts with master calendars, different judges may be assigned to hear specific types of hearings. One judge may hear shelter care hearings, another review hearing, and another termination of parental rights cases. This method ensures that, as a case moves forward, different judges will be involved. Thus, the common factor in juvenile courts with master calendars is that, over time, a number of different judges will conduct hearings in a single case.

By contrast, an *individual calendar* means that once a case is filed, the same judge keeps the case and holds any necessary hearings until the case is concluded. There are many courts that use calendaring arrangements that are somewhere in between a pure master or individual calendar. In such courts, for example, one judge might conduct shelter care and pretrial hearings and another judge takes over after that.

From the perspective of the child welfare administrator, there are a number of important advantages to having the court use an individual calendar system. With individual calendars, the parties feel more connected with the judge and therefore less alienated. They are more likely to obey court orders knowing they will return to the same judge.

Because the judge knows the case better, parents and their attorneys are less able to use the same arguments or excuses more than once. When the case stays with the same judge, it is easier to develop a stable case plan.

Another important difference in the organization of juvenile courts nationally is the placement of the court in the particular state's judicial hierarchy. A trial court's place on the judicial hierarchy is based upon the types of cases that it hears.

Higher level trial courts, often referred to as courts of *general jurisdiction*, are empowered to hear all types of cases including felony criminal cases and expensive civil cases. Lower level trial courts, often referred to as courts of *limited jurisdiction*, typically hear only criminal misdemeanor cases and civil cases involving a limited sum of money.

If the juvenile court is classified as a limited jurisdiction (lower level) trial court, its judges are at the bottom of the judicial ladder. On the other hand, if the juvenile court is part of the court of general jurisdiction, the judges are higher on the judicial ladder. It is easier to have stable judicial appointments when the juvenile court is at the level of the court of general jurisdiction.

In some of the states where the juvenile court is a court of limited jurisdiction, appeals from juvenile court require a retrial by the court of general jurisdiction. In such states, it generally is more difficult for agencies to establish legal precedent.

To set precedent that will be binding on local juvenile court judges, an agency may need to retry a case in the court of general jurisdiction and *then* (assuming that the agency also loses on retrial) to take the case to the appeals court.

A similar situation emerges in some states where the juvenile court is a part of the court of general jurisdiction, but in which subordinate judicial officials are used to try abuse and neglect cases. In courts using "referees," "commissioners," or "hearing officers" to try cases, dissatisfied parties must first have the case reheard by a judge before pursuing a further appeal. This extra step may slow down the judicial decision-making process, especially the final determination in a case, such as the termination of parental rights.

On the other hand, some states using "referees" or other "non-judges" to try cases do not require the case to be retried when appealed. Some states require a judge to review the record of the case, which involves less work and less time than a retrial.

More states are implementing specialized family courts, in which judges hear only child welfare cases and other cases related to families. Whether these courts and their judges are equal in status to the court of general jurisdiction affects how long judges remain in a family court.

In states without family courts, it is common to rotate judges in and out of juvenile court. This rotation prevents the special recruitment of judges as experts in juvenile and family matters. The frequency of the rotation is important. While in some places a judge might remain within the juvenile court for several years, in others, judges are rotated in and out every few months. As a result, judges do not become knowledgeable about child welfare law or practice.

In some courts where referees or other judicial subordinates carry much of the burden of child welfare cases, the referees are actually more knowledgeable than the judges regarding child welfare law and practice. This situation most often occurs when judges rotate in and out of the court but referee positions are more stable.

Key Juvenile Court Problems and Reforms

In recent years, juvenile court proceedings have been burdened by two major developments. The workload has increased and the issues faced by the courts have become more complex.

Juvenile court workloads have increased partly because caseloads continue to rise. In addition, the workload has been compounded by the added number of hearings and lawyers typically involved in a single case. Caseloads can vary sharply among different courts, often even within the same state.

Likewise, there is some variation in the number of hearings and lawyers per case. For example, review hearings by the court are far more frequent in some places than others. In some courts, there usually are no more than two lawyers while in others three or four are typical.

The effect of increasing judicial workloads is that many court calendars have been overloaded as a result. When court dockets are jammed, caseworkers usually spend more time sitting around the courtroom waiting for hearings. In addition, it takes longer to schedule hearings and cases are more often repeatedly continued.

Juvenile courts need to develop and implement caseload standards for child maltreatment and foster care cases. These caseloads need to be low enough for juvenile courts to deal with the additional parties and conduct the additional hearings. At the same time, as more fully discussed below, courts need to adopt management reforms to cope with their caseloads.

Legal issues have become more complex in child welfare cases because of the concept of permanency planning. Courts, like agencies, are now charged with achieving permanency for children in foster care. Because of the intensified involvement of courts after a child is placed into foster care, the law and procedure has become more complex.

State statutes are more elaborate and there is more case law (legal precedent from appeals courts). Judges are expected to know how to deal with cases involving such issues as psychological bonding, independent living services, adoption subsidy, and the placement of children with special needs.

As the result of increased interest in children's issues and the availability of grant funds, such as the Court Improvement Project Grant and the Adoption Opportunities Grant, many juvenile courts have introduced wide-ranging reforms. You should be aware of ongoing reform efforts in your state and take advantage of opportunities to participate in various task forces where appropriate.

Juvenile court reforms have many facets, and some of the major areas of reform are addressed below. For more details about court reforms and to see what reforms your state is implementing, see the *Court Improvement Progress Report National Summary and State Summaries*, located online at www.abanet.org/child/cipcatalog/home.html.

Model courts and pilot projects. Numerous states have used Court Improvement Project funds or other grant funds to establish model courts and pilot projects designed to improve the handling of abuse and neglect cases. These model courts take various forms, including family courts, drug and treatment courts, cluster courts in rural areas, and other specialized dockets. Other pilot projects include review systems to monitor court compliance with federal and state time frames and use of courtroom teams to provide consistency in representation.

Technology. With major advancements in computer and Internet technologies over the past decade, more courts are becoming automated. Such automation can take the form of laptops in the courtroom, giving the judge the capability to set hearings in advance and provide the parties with orders when they leave the courtroom. Some states are experimenting with online calendaring as well, allowing other parties in the case limited access.

Computer technology has allowed many courts to develop case tracking and management systems. For example, Georgia has developed a case plan system that allows caseworkers and judges to access individual case plans through a password system. This system allows the parties to leave the courtroom with a completed case plan instead of having to wait 30 days. Other states are considering electronic filing of reports.

One area that can allow for the direct participation of the agency is data integration between courts and child welfare agencies. Many states are considering or implementing interfaces between the agency data collection system and the court's system, so more accurate data can be produced and better compliance with federal and state law achieved.

Other technologies allow for better production of court transcription or video conferencing.

Most recently, several states were awarded federal Strengthening Abuse and Neglect Courts in America: Management Information Systems (SANCA-MIS) grants. These grants, authorized through 2005, are being used to enhance case management systems and improve performance measurement. Through such improvements, participating states will obtain better data to track timeliness of cases.

Alternative dispute resolution. The past decade has also seen an increase in the use of various alternative dispute resolution techniques. Mediation and family group conferencing are being implemented in many states. These programs can help reduce time spent in court and the adversarial nature of proceedings, ultimately benefiting the child.

Parent education and support programs. A number of state courts have produced brochures and videos designed to inform parents of their rights and responsibilities in the court process. A few states have developed mentoring programs, where a parent who previously had a child in foster care but has had their child returned works with other parents. These materials and programs can assist your caseworkers with parent education and help parents understand the impact of ASFA's shortened time frames.

Manuals and guides. Many states have developed manuals and guides designed to help all stakeholders, including caseworkers. Iowa and New York are two states that have developed manuals designed specifically to guide caseworkers. These resources can be invaluable to the various parties as a way to achieve *best practice*.

The future of Court Improvement efforts. Since the inception of the Court Improvement Project, great strides have been made. However, there are more improvements that should be achieved. Excellence in child protection cases has some key features, such as timeliness of the process, skilled and knowledgeable practitioners for all parties, thoroughness of reports and hearings, procedural fairness, and fair treatment of parties.

To achieve excellence in child protection cases, specific areas within these broader categories still need significant work. For example, the continued development and refinement of quality assurance through performance measurement is vital to determining whether the process is timely. Development of reasonable workload calculations and standards for both judges and attorneys will ensure skilled and knowledgeable practitioners are handling these cases.

Long-range planning is necessary to institutionalize and guarantee continuation of successful projects. When you offer your skills as an agency administrator to these efforts, you are demonstrating the agency's commitment to an improved process. You assist courts in becoming well-run and efficient. Ultimately, the children in your agency's care benefit because permanency is achieved in a more timely fashion.

5

Improving Agency Legal Representation

There was so much help our attorneys could have been giving us. But we didn't get that help until we realized what we were missing, and then asked for it — and then demanded it!

Without good legal representation, it is difficult or impossible for agencies to develop a sound working relationship with the court. Good attorneys are needed not only to present effective cases in court, but also to provide legal training to workers and to help the agency work out administrative and logistical problems with the court.

Many agency administrators have very low expectations of their attorneys and accept mediocre legal representation without complaint. In fact, many child welfare agencies tolerate a kind of legal representation that would not be acceptable in the private sector. Imagine the following absurd situation involving the mythical Aardvark Corporation, a manufacturer of engine components:

> Aardvark management is the defendant in a large number of lawsuits claiming that its products fail to meet contract specifications. Many corporate officials are being called to testify, but attorneys representing Aardvark are willing to meet with them just five minutes before court hearings begin. The law firm says that its workload is too high to spend more time with the corporate officers before they testify.
>
> Corporation attorneys persist in negotiating settlements to lawsuits without prior approval of the corporation president. Sometimes the

attorneys refuse to defend the corporation's products from lawsuits because they feel that the products were poorly designed.

Aardvark would like its attorneys to help it improve its sales contracts to prevent future lawsuits. However, the law firm says that it doesn't have time to improve the contracts.

This example is absurd because no corporation would tolerate a law firm that failed to prepare witnesses for court, settled lawsuits without consulting corporation management, declined to represent the corporation's position when it was legally defensible, or refused to give the corporation advice on how to prevent future lawsuits.

Yet, many child welfare agencies find themselves in situations roughly analogous to that of the hypothetical Aardvark Corporation. Some child welfare attorneys do not meet with caseworkers well in advance of court hearings (or do not even attend all court hearings); are not willing to meet with the agency for case planning conferences; do not provide training for agency staff; and do not help design agency forms and procedures for dealing with the court.

Such deficiencies in legal representation should be as rare in child welfare cases as in they are the private sector. Besides representing the agency in court, helping workers prepare cases, sitting in on case conferences, and providing training, the agency needs the help of its lawyers in communicating and dealing with the court on systemic issues. Systemic problems often deal with legal and procedural technicalities, and agencies need their attorneys to explain the issues and help to fashion solutions.

Because of the importance of agency legal representation, it is a good idea periodically to conduct a careful self-evaluation of one's legal services. Two useful tools to help with such a self-evaluation are M. Laver, *Foundations for Success: Strengthening Your Agency Attorney Office,* (ABA 1999) and E. Segal, *Evaluating and Improving Child Welfare Agency Legal Representation: Self-Assessment and Commentary* (ABA 1985). Many issues discussed here are also addressed in these publications.

Demanding Better Services from Attorneys and Making the Issue an Agency Priority

Agency administrators faced with inadequate legal representation may feel powerless to improve the situation. Unlike the Aardvark Corporation, they feel that they are not free to fire or direct their attorneys.

There are understandable reasons why agency administrators sometimes decline to use lawyers. Some agency lawyers are very cautious and prefer to tell administrators that they cannot do things that are good for children. For example, in one state, attorneys advised the agency not to allow 16-year-olds in foster care to obtain drivers' licenses instead of advising it how to reduce its liability and help foster parents place children on their own liability policies. Some agency lawyers seem more involved in raising technicalities and problems than helping the agency overcome legal barriers to serving children.

The important thing for administrators to keep in mind is that there are things that can be done to improve agency legal representation. Others have succeeded. Many administrators have been able to obtain additional legal help, to redefine the duties of their lawyers, to replace incompetent or unhelpful lawyers, or even to change who represents their agencies.

To accomplish these things, the administrator needs to be able to make a good case for the need for change and then to make the issue a priority and be persistent in pursuing it. A good starting point is to formulate a clear idea of what improvements in legal representation are needed.

Specific Services That Attorneys Should Provide in Child Welfare Cases

Agency administrators need to understand the full range of services that their attorneys should provide and the value of such services. The following are things that child welfare agency attorneys should do to help agencies achieve good results in court:

- ❖ Be present and actively represent the agency during all court hearings.

- ❖ Confer with the caseworker about each case prior to the day of each hearing.

- ❖ Thoroughly plan and prepare for contested hearings, having face-to-face conferences with the caseworker at least two days in advance.

- ❖ Maintain regular office hours at the agency, to be available to talk to caseworkers (e.g., at a specified time each week).

- ❖ Meet periodically with the agency (e.g., at least once every six months) to review each case, to make sure that each case is legally on track.

- ❖ Train agency caseworkers about legal issues and about the court.

- ❖ Bring cases to court when the agency wishes, so long as there is a valid legal basis for doing so.

- ❖ Always obtain agency permission before reaching settlements.

- ❖ Have the same attorney stay with each individual case from the time that the case is first brought to court until the involvement of the court is ended.

The following are services that attorneys should provide to help make the legal process work better:

- ❖ help the agency work with the court to address systemic issues and problems;

- ❖ help to develop local forms for agency reports and court orders; and

- ❖ help obtain favorable court procedures, forms, and rules at the state level by working with the state Court Improvement Project, Administrative Office of the Courts, Supreme Court, or Court Rules Committees.

Finally, the attorney should help make sure that the agency's regulations and policy manual are consistent with federal laws and regulations as well as state statutes. The attorney should make special efforts to make sure that the agency is not placing unnecessary burdens upon itself based on misunderstandings of what the law requires.

If your agency is not receiving all of these types of services, it is receiving incomplete representation. If these services are done halfheartedly or poorly, it is receiving inadequate representation.

Increasingly, states are developing practice standards for agency attorneys. Standards can help improve the quality of representation and the consistency of practice in your office and your state. For a detailed discussion of the process for developing standards and the important information to include in those standards, see Chapter 1 in M. Laver, *Foundations for Success: Strengthening Your Agency Attorney Office* (ABA 1999).

In addition, the ABA recently developed model standards based on the information discussed in *Foundations for Success*. *The Standards of Practice for Lawyers Representing Child Welfare Agencies* are divided into five categories:

- Definitions,
- the Role of the Agency Attorney,
- Fulfilling the Obligations,
- Ethical and Practice Considerations, and
- Administrative Responsibilities.

The Standards can be found at www.abanet.org/child/documents.agencyattystandards.pdf.

Remember, standards cannot be met if your attorneys are handling too many cases. You may need to address the issue of excessive caseloads while proceeding with standards.

Things for Administrators to Do to Get the Type of Legal Representation That Agencies Need

Show your attorneys the above list. Discuss it with them. Ask them which of the above services they are able to perform, why they cannot do more, and what it would take for them to perform all of the services. Put in writing what kinds of additional services and help that you need from your attorneys.

It may be appropriate to propose changes to someone higher in authority than the attorneys who actually represent you in court. For example, depending on how your agency is represented, it might be an attorney at a higher level within the attorney general's office, the county counsel's office, the county commissioners, and so forth.

If your agency enters into contracts for legal services, then one way for the agency to obtain better legal services is to negotiate different terms in future contracts. That is, if the agency is not receiving a needed service from its contract attorneys, it may choose to specify in the next contract that such service shall be provided.

Here are some examples of terms that could be inserted into a contract between a state agency and an office that provides legal services for the agency:

- ❖ Attorneys will submit court orders and forms that comply with federal laws, including ASFA, and Titles IV-B and IV-E of the Social Security Act.

- ❖ Attorneys will provide one full day of annual training for local caseworkers.

- ❖ Attorneys will be available to meet with caseworkers at the agency office for __ hours at a regular time each week.

- ❖ Attorneys will attend annual case planning conferences in every case.

❖ Attorneys will follow the directions of the agency in deciding whether to initiate cases whenever there is a reasonable legal basis for the case.

❖ Attorneys will not negotiate agreements without the approval of the agency and, except for issues of legal tactics, will accept case objectives as established by the agency.

❖ Attorneys will attend child welfare training conferences on child welfare law on an annual basis.

❖ Attorneys will be available outside working hours to provide legal services during emergencies.

❖ Attorneys shall be assigned to handle child welfare cases for at least two-year time periods.

❖ The agency shall be permitted to participate in new attorneys' recruitment and selection.

❖ New attorneys shall, to the extent possible, have prior experience, training, and a demonstrated interest in the area of child welfare.

❖ Attorneys shall be assigned to handle child welfare cases on at least a half-time basis.

In short, if the agency is paying for the attorneys, it should be assertive regarding the services that they are to provide.

Agencies that enter into contracts for legal services need to be careful about contracting for a set percentage of an attorney's time without specifying the hours to be worked. If, for example, an agency is contracting with an attorney on a half-time basis and it has any concern about the amount of time that the attorney will give the agency, specify a minimum number of hours to be worked and require the attorney to provide a precise account of time worked to the agency. This obligation should be specified in the contract.

Hiring new attorneys gives agencies an excellent opportunity to set new guidelines and to set a new tone for its legal representation. There are many aspects to the hiring process and the following ideas are discussed in greater detail in Chapter 2 of *Foundations for Success: Strengthening Your Agency Attorney Office*.

- ❖ Create a hiring committee when seeking new candidates. Include individuals who will work with the new attorney(s) as well as individual(s) who have the authority to hire.

- ❖ Develop hiring criteria that takes into consideration educational and professional experience, experience in and commitment to the field, the needs of your agency and your community, the ability to get along with many types of people, the ability to think creatively, and the ability to handle stress.

- ❖ Create a job description and adequately post the description in locations likely to attract good candidates, such as law schools, bar association publications, and child welfare periodicals.

- ❖ Screen your candidates, develop an interview format, and proceed with the interviews. Ask open-ended questions to obtain information from the candidate, provide information about the position (both positive and negative), and allow the candidate to ask questions. Provide information about your hiring process and timetable for a final decision.

- ❖ The final step before extending an offer is to be sure and check the candidate's references. Follow your human resources department's process for extending an offer.

The agency's expectations of the attorney can be set forth in writing, either by contract as described above or in the form of a memorandum to the attorney. Besides specifying the attorney's duties in writing, there are a number of things that the agency can do to help ensure that it receives good representation from the new attorney:

- ❖ If possible, let the attorney know that he or she is responsible to the child welfare director (someone operating at a very high level within the agency who has the authority to hire and fire the attorney).

- Set up regular evaluations of the attorney, perhaps at six-month intervals. Factors to be considered in these evaluations, as well a sample evaluation, are found in Chapter 4 of *Foundations for Success*.

- Expect the attorney to make a slow start, and make sure that the agency provides good moral support, preferably by providing the attorney with another experienced attorney as a mentor.

- Provide good staff support for the attorney, including paralegal and secretarial support.

- Provide the attorney with good equipment, including a computer, computer printer, and fax machine, as well as Internet access.

- Set aside some time for the attorney to become familiar with state statutes and case law and to read more general child welfare literature.

- Provide the attorney with a list of experts to consult and use as witnesses in difficult cases.

- Rather than expecting the attorney to handle a large caseload immediately, allow the attorney to gain experience in preparing cases thoroughly.

- Encourage experienced and highly skilled caseworkers to set up brown bag lunches with the attorney to discuss child welfare issues.

If there are not enough attorneys to provide essential services to the agency, administrators should think of ways to seek funding for additional attorneys. This effort should be made even if the funding is to go to an entity other than the agency. However, if the funding is not under the agency's control, try to get explicit written commitments (e.g., through memoranda) from the other office that it will provide specific types of services to the agency with the additional funding.

Sometimes, getting funding for attorneys reduces funding for other agency activities. If this outcome is possible, administrators need to ask themselves honestly which funding is most urgently needed. For example, if there are great delays in the agency's legally freeing children for adoption due to a lack of attorneys, more attorneys should be a high agency priority.

Agencies should object when existing attorneys are not doing their best. For example, the agency may choose to complain when:

- ❖ attorneys are not providing the full range of services to the agency that are described above, although able to provide the services;

- ❖ attorneys refuse or are reluctant to pursue appeals;

- ❖ attorneys refuse to pursue meritorious cases based on their independent analysis of what is best;

- ❖ attorneys reach unilateral settlements of cases without consent of the caseworker or supervisor;

- ❖ attorneys are discourteous; or

- ❖ attorneys fail to consistently meet in advance with caseworkers to prepare cases, e.g., one attorney does and another does not.

Agencies should set up an informal grievance mechanism to address problems between attorneys and agency staff. This mechanism should allow:

- ❖ caseworkers and agency managers to address problems with attorneys,

- ❖ attorneys to address problems with agency staff, and

- ❖ attorneys occasionally to question the decisions of caseworkers and supervisors.

Beyond correcting specific problems with attorneys, agency administrators may need to develop a strategy for getting rid of attorneys who are ineffective or difficult to get along with — after informal conversations with the attorneys and their direct superior have been unsuccessful. After verbal complaints, administrators should be prepared to send memoranda of complaint to the attorney, with very specific examples involving more than one caseworker. Such memoranda should only be sent out from a high level within the agency.

Assuming that such memoranda to an attorney do not work and the problem persists, the administrator should follow up with written complaints to the attorney's superiors with further specific examples. The examples should explain how the attorney's conduct adversely affected a child. Consider the following example:

> On May 1, Attorney Schmedly requested a continuance of the <u>Audry Z.</u> case because of alleged witness unavailability. In fact, the witness was unavailable only because Attorney Schmedly had not notified her of the trial date initially. Attorney Schmedly also pointed out to the caseworker that he welcomed the continuance because he was not ready for trial.
>
> Based on Schmedly's request, the judge continued the case for four additional months. This delay means four additional months that Audry must needlessly await adoption. Audry already feels extremely tense about the case and since the continuance, has been asking whether the court will ever decide, and has had several nightmares about the trial.

There should be a number of examples like the one above, and it should be clear that attorney Schmedly was not excused by an unreasonably high caseload.

While administrators and supervisors should document problems with attorneys, when necessary, agencies that employ their own attorneys should not assign employment decisions to persons low on the organizational command structure.

Inexperienced managers may not appreciate how legal ethics may constrain an attorney from bringing a particular case or adopting a particular tactic. Consider the following hypothetical example:

> A local child welfare manager wants to submit psychological reports only to the judge and not to the party against whom they are being used. The supervising agency attorney refuses, stating that this practice would violate due process and state discovery rules. The disagreement develops

into a confrontation that threatens the employment of the supervising attorney.

To resolve the issue, a more senior manager intervenes and consults with the state attorney general, who confirms that the legal position of the supervising attorney is correct. This intercession protects the attorney from having to choose between continued employment and unethical practice.

Many administrators do not fully grasp the importance of providing adequate equipment, facilities, and support staff to the agency's attorneys. These are essential to obtaining the types of representation advocated here. Remember that attorneys generate (or should generate) a tremendous number of documents in the course of their work: petitions, motions, legal arguments, briefs, memoranda, and many others.

Skilled paralegals and support staff not only can perform their tasks less expensively than attorneys, but also can help relieve attorneys' stress and boredom. They can take time to help caseworkers organize their cases into a form useful for the attorneys. The use of paralegal and other specialized staff is discussed in more detail in chapter 2, *General Strategies for Working with Courts*.

Finally, agencies need to take an active role in providing training for their attorneys. This topic is discussed in detail in chapter 2, *General Strategies for Working with Courts*.

Systemic Issues in Legal Representation for Child Welfare Agencies

Agency administrators should be aware of the variety of types of legal representation for child welfare agencies. Here are some possibilities:

❖ a legal branch of state government (such as the attorney general's office);

❖ a locally elected prosecutor (such as a district attorney or state's attorney);

❖ a unit of attorneys who are employees of the child welfare agency;

❖ a private attorney or firm working on contract for the agency; and

❖ a combination of the above, such as a prosecutor for abuse and neglect trials, but a state agency attorney for termination of parental rights cases.

All things being equal, the recommended form of legal representation is a unit of attorneys who are employed by the agency, who represent it in court, and who help it to formulate policy. This recommendation assumes, however, that the agency will be politically able to recruit and select the most highly qualified attorneys.

Many state agencies are saddled with attorneys who serve as policy advisors but who neither are involved in juvenile court trial work nor have experience in child welfare issues. Some of these attorneys do a good job, but their lack of experience and lack of any occasional juvenile court involvement is a disadvantage. Some state agencies have solved this problem by having their attorneys provide litigation help in occasional difficult juvenile court cases.

Some agencies hire attorneys on a part-time basis or allow full-time attorneys to represent private clients on the side. Many agency attorneys who are permitted also to represent private paying clients concentrate more on building their private practice than on providing strong representation for the agency. This type of arrangement is not recommended.

There are special problems when local prosecutors represent agencies in rural areas. Often, local prosecutors cannot devote a high enough proportion of their time to gain expertise in child welfare issues. New prosecutors may not have supervisors or peers who can instruct them in child welfare law and practice.

States that use local attorneys to represent the agency at early stages but use state attorneys to handle termination of parental rights cases also face special difficulties. The attorneys handling the early stages of the case may not take steps to prepare for the possible eventuality of termination, such as by resolving the legal status of unwed fathers, notifying missing parents, bringing in relatives early, making an accurate court record of the original abuse, and so forth. States in which different attorneys handle different stages of the case must make extra efforts to strengthen communications and mutual training involving state and local attorneys.

6

Conclusion

> The biggest mistake we made in dealing with courts was underestimating our ability to solve problems together.

It is not always easy to resolve problems with courts. Lawyers and judges speak an arcane language and follow a set of rules that are obscure to persons not legally trained. Attorneys and judges sometimes seem abrasive and domineering.

In addition, some of the very attorneys who are supposed to represent the child welfare agency may act like they are part of a rival bureaucracy. Some do not feel invested in achieving the mission of the child welfare agency. Finally, there may be resistance within the agency to working with courts, because of the inevitable tension between agencies and judges.

In the face of these obstacles, administrators need to maintain a positive focus. It is tempting to give up when faced with difficulties with courts. It is easier to give in to feelings of alienation from the courts and to adopt cynical attitudes than to analyze and attempt to solve problems.

Administrators need to explain to staff that passive acceptance of one's difficulties with courts is self-defeating. There are three critical points for staff to keep in mind:

❖ First, when courts do not function properly, not only are agencies inconvenienced, but children and families also suffer. Courts make decisions vital to children's lives and futures — whether to remove them from the home; whether to allow them to be returned home; whether to approve the case plan (in some states); and whether to legally free them for adoption. Mistaken decisions can result in injury, death, or needless family disruption. Delayed decisions can interfere with normal child development. Unnecessary demands on agency time interfere with the agency's efforts to assist families. In sum, the quality of the court process has a profound effect on children's quality of life.

- ❖ Second, some juvenile courts function far better than others in child maltreatment cases. Some have far fewer delays than others; some are far more expert in child welfare issues than others; some conduct far more thorough hearings than others; some have taken steps to avoid needless inconvenience to caseworkers. Moreover, some agencies and courts operate in relative sync in their case decisions. Thus, much can be done to improve the quality of court proceedings in child welfare cases and to make the proceedings more accommodating to agencies.

- ❖ Third, agencies do have a great influence on the quality and responsiveness of court proceedings in child welfare cases. Agencies alert courts to problems, work out solutions, and advocate for fundamental reforms. As described in this book, there are many specific steps that agencies can take to improve their advocacy and working relationships with their courts.

It is not enough, however, for agencies simply to make occasional attempts toward improvement. Many agencies have attempted but failed to resolve problems with their courts. To be successful in working with the courts, agencies must develop a well-reasoned strategy and give it top priority. This strategy includes identifying the precise problems with the courts, prioritizing them, and developing an overall step-by-step plan of action.

Agencies need to maintain an optimistic attitude about their eventual success. They must be ready to invest their time, resources, and political capital. To solve especially difficult problems, agencies must be prepared to continue their efforts over a period of years.

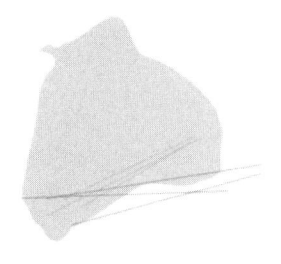

About the Authors

Mark Hardin, J.D., is the director of Child Welfare for the ABA Center on Children and the Law in Washington, D.C. In this capacity, he conducts research and provides consultation and training throughout the United States. He is the author of many books and other materials on legal and judicial issues in child welfare. Among his awards are the Adoption 2002 Excellence Award (category of judicial improvement), U.S. Secretary of Health and Human Services and the Outstanding Legal Advocacy Award, National Association of Counsel for Children. He has worked in child welfare and children's law for 29 years and received his law degree from the University of Oregon.

Diane Boyd Rauber, M.Ed., J.D., is a specialist in child welfare court improvement and related issues, and author/researcher. She has authored, co-authored, and edited numerous ABA and Resource Center publications, including *Court Improvement Progress Report* (ABA 2004), *A Judge's Guide: Making Child-Centered Decisions in Custody Cases* (ABA 2001), and *Making Sense of the ASFA Regulations: A Roadmap for Effective Implementation* (2001). She received her master's degree in special education from the University of Pittsburgh and her law degree from the Catholic University of America.

About the Author

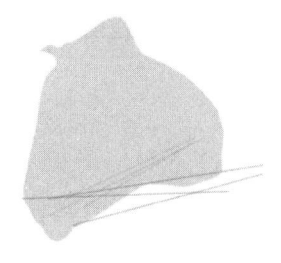

Appendix: Where to Go for Additional Advice and Information

Judicial and Bar Organizations

ABA Center on Children and the Law
740 15th Street NW 9th Floor
Washington, DC 20005
Telephone: (202) 662-1000

Contact: Mark Hardin
(markhardin@staff.abanet.org)

Website:
http://www.abanet.org/child/home2.html

National Association of Counsel for Children
1825 Marion Street, Suite 242
Denver, CO 80218

Telephone: 1 (888) 828-NACC

Contact: Marvin Ventrell
(ventrell.marvin@tchden.org)

Website: http://naccchildlaw.org/

National Center for Juvenile Justice
701 Fifth Avenue, Suite 3000
Pittsburgh, PA 15219

Telephone: (412) 227-6950

Contact: Hunter Hurst (ncjj@ncjj.org)

Website: http://www.ncjj.org/

National Center for State Courts
300 Newport Avenue
Williamsburg, VA 23185

Telephone: (757) 259-1823

Contact: Victor E. Flango, Ph.D.
(gflango@ncsc.dni.us)

Website: http://www.ncsconline.org/

National Council of Juvenile and Family Court Judges
P.O. Box 8970
Reno, NV 89507

Telephone: (775) 327-5300

Contact: Christine Bailey

Website: http://www.ncjfcj.org/

Appendix: Where to Go for Additional Advice and Information

Federal Contacts

For federal technical assistance and interpretations of policies under the Adoption Assistance and Child Welfare Act (P.L. 96-272), contact the United States Children's Bureau. The Children's Bureau is a unit of the Administration on Children, Youth and Families (AYCF), which itself is part of the Administration for Children and Families (ACF) of the Department of Health and Human Services (DHHS).

Children's Bureau contacts are as follows:

National Office

United States Children's Bureau
DHHS/ACF/ACYF
330 C Street, SW
Washington, DC 20447

Telephone: (202) 205-8618

Contacts: Emily Cooke (Court Improvement Program); Jerry Milner (Child and Family Services Reviews)

Website:
http://www.acf.hhs.gov/programs/cb/

Regional Offices

Region I (Massachusetts, New Hampshire, Rhode Island, Maine, Vermont)
DHHS/ACF/ACYF
JFK Federal Building, Room 2000
Boston, MA 02203

Telephone: (617) 565-1020

Contacts: Hugh Galligan, Regional Administrator (hgalligan@acf.hhs.gov); Veronica Melendez, Massachusetts (617-565-1148); Julie Monro, New Hampshire (617-565-3671); Amy Lockhart, Rhode Island (617-565-1135); Nancy Pickett, Vermont (617-565-2460)

Website:
http://www.acf.hhs.gov/programs/region1/index.htm

Region II (New Jersey, New York, Puerto Rico, Virgin Islands)
DHHS/ACF/ACYF
26 Federal Plaza, Room 4114
New York, NY 10278

Telephone: (212) 264-2890

Contacts: Mary Ann Higgins, Regional Administrator (mhiggins@acf.hhs.gov); Carolyn Baker, New Jersey (212-264-2890 X140); Evelyn Torres-Ortega, Virgin Islands (212-264-2890 X146); Shari Brown, New York (212-264-2890 X125)

Website:
http://www.acf.hhs.gov/programs/region2/index.htm

Region III (Delaware, District of Columbia, Maryland, Pennsylvania, Virginia, West Virginia)
DHHS/ACF/ACYF
150 S. Independence
Mall West – Suite 864
Philadelphia, PA 19106-3499

Telephone: (215) 861-4000

Contacts: David Lett, Regional Administrator (dlett@acf.hhs.gov); Alan Ademski, Pennsylvania (215-861-4035); Gary Koch, Delaware, West Virginia (215-861-4022); Delores Smith, Maryland (215-861-4037); Christine Craig, Virginia/ D.C. (215-861-4065)

Website:
http://www.acf.hhs.gov/programs/region3/index.htm

Region IV (Alabama, Florida, Georgia, Kentucky, Mississippi, North Carolina, South Carolina, Tennessee)
DHHS/ACF/ACYF
Atlanta Federal Center
61 Forsyth Street SW, Suite 4M60
Atlanta, GA 30303

Telephone: (404) 562-2900

Contacts: Carlis V. Williams, Regional Administrator (cvwilliams@acf.hhs.gov); Ann Fontaine, Alabama/South Carolina (404-562-2949); Kunle Baoku, Georgia (404-562-2949); John Margolis, Florida (404-562-2904); Carola Pike, Kentucky/Mississippi (404-562-2907); Fred Ritchie, North Carolina/Tennessee (404-562-2902)

Website:
http://www.acf.hhs.gov/programs/region4/index.htm

Region V (Illinois, Indiana, Michigan, Minnesota, Ohio, Wisconsin)
DHHS/ACF/ACYF
233 N. Michigan Avenue, Suite 400
Chicago, IL 60601

Telephone: (312) 353-4237

Contacts: Joyce A. Thomas, Regional Administrator (acf.chicago@acf.hhs.gov); Barbara Putyra, Michigan (312-353-1786); Ron Stevens, Illinois (312-886-5036); Len Tufo, Indiana (312-353-7484); Mary Doran, Ohio (312-886-4597); Christie Guthrie, Minnesota (312-886-4916); Patris Shirells, Wisconsin (312-353-6450)

Website:
http://www.acf.hhs.gov/programs/region5/index.htm

Region VI (Arkansas, Louisiana, New Mexico, Oklahoma, Texas)
DHHS/ACF/ACYF
1301 Young Street, Suite 914
Dallas, TX 75202

Telephone: (213) 767-9648

Contacts: Leon McCowan, Regional Administrator (dallas@acf.hhs.gov); Judy Baggett, Tribal Lead/All States (214-767-8078); Amy Grissom, Arkansas (214-767-4542); Laurie Hagedorn, Oklahoma (214-767-8029); T.J. Jones, Louisiana (214-767-4158);

Patricia Newlin, New Mexico (214-767-1971); Joseph Woodard, Texas (214-767-4958)

Website: http://www.acf.hhs.gov/programs/region6/index.htm

Region VII (Iowa, Kansas, Missouri, Nebraska)
DHHS/ACF/ACYF
Federal Office Building, Room 276
601 E 12th Street
Kansas City, MO 64106

Telephone: (816) 426-2223

Contacts: Linda Lewis, Regional Administrator (llewis@acf.hhs.gov); Mary McKee, Nebraska (816-426-2263); Ann Burds, Missouri (816-426-2260); Sue Bradfield, Iowa (816-426-2261)

Website: http://www.acf.hhs.gov/programs/region7/index.htm

Region VIII (Colorado, Montana, North Dakota, South Dakota, Utah, Wyoming)
DHHS/ACF/ACYF
Federal Office Building
1961 Stout Street, 9th Floor
Denver, CO 80294-3538

Telephone: (303) 844-3100

Contacts: Thomas Sullivan, Regional Administrator (tsullivan@acf.hhs.gov); Gloria Montgomery, Wyoming/Colorado (303-844-1181); Eric Busch, Montana/North Dakota (303-844-1134); Kevin Gomez, Utah/South Dakota (303-844-1147)

Website: http://www.acf.hhs.gov/programs/region8/index.htm

Region IX (Arizona, California, Hawaii, Nevada)
DHHS/ACF/ACYF
50 United Nations Plaza, Room 450
San Francisco, CA 94102

Telephone: (415) 437-8400

Contacts: Sharon Fujii, Regional Administrator (sfujii@acf.hhs.gov); Katherine Aguilar, Nevada (415-437-8543); Corinne Corson, California (415-437-8661); Tim Fox, California (415-437-8660); Lynda Garcia (Revelynda), California/Arizona Tribes (415-437-8546); Anita Grandpre, Hawaii (415-437-8424); Kim Relph, Arizona/Nevada (415-437-8485); Pat Pianko, California (415-437-8462); Debra Samples, California (415-437-8626); Dennis Setlock, Arizona (415-437-8541); Rick Wever, Arizona Tribes (415-437-8460)

Website: http://www.acf.hhs.gov/programs/region9/index.htm

Appendix: Where to Go for Additional Advice and Information

Region X (Alaska, Idaho, Oregon, Washington)
DHHS/ACF/ACYF
Blanchard Plaza
2201 Sixth Avenue
Room 610-M/S RX-70
Seattle, WA 98121

Telephone: (206) 615-2547

Contact: Steve Henigson, Regional Administrator (shenigson@acf.hhs.gov); John Henderson, Oregon (206-615-2482); Carol Overbeck, Washington (206-615-2602); Lois Ward, Alaska (206-615-2603); Jennifer Zanella, Idaho (206-615-2604)

Website:
http://www.acf.hhs.gov/programs/region10/index.htm

Appendix: Where to Go for Additional Advice and Information

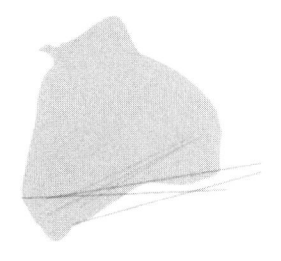

Bibliography

Administration for Children and Families, U.S. Dept. of Health and Human Services, *Child Welfare Policy Manual* Section 8.3A.12 (online at http://www.acf.hhs.gov/programs/cb/laws/cwpm/policy.jsp).

American Bar Association, *Model Rules of Judicial Conduct* (Chicago: 1990).

American Bar Association, *Model Rules of Judicial Conduct* (Chicago: 1972).

American Bar Association, *Standards of Practice for Lawyers Representing Child Welfare Agencies* (Washington: 2004)(online at http://www.abanet.org/child/documents/agencyattystandards.pdf).

Baker, Debra Ratterman, et al. *Making Sense of the ASFA Regulations: A Roadmap for Effective Implementation* (Washington: American Bar Association, D. Boyd Rauber ed. 2001).

Boyer, Bruce A. "Jurisdictional Conflicts Between Juvenile Courts and Child Welfare Agencies: The Uneasy Relationship Between Institutional Co-Parents," 54 *Md.L.Rev.* 377 (1995).

Edwards, Hon. Leonard P. "The Juvenile Court and the Role of the Juvenile Court Judge," *Juvenile and Family Court Journal*, Vol. 43, No. 2, pp. 1-45 (1992).

Feller, Jane, et al. *Working with the Courts in Child Protection* (Washington: National Center on Child Abuse and Neglect 1992). This book can be obtained through the National Clearinghouse on Abuse and Neglect Information (online at www.nccanch.acf.hhs.gov/).

Fiermonte, Cecilia, and Jennifer L. Renne. *Making It Permanent: Reasonable Efforts to Finalize Permanency Plans for Foster Children* (Washington: American Bar Association, C. Sandt ed. 2002).

Hardin, Mark. *How and Why to Involve the Courts in Your Child and Family Services Review (CFSR): Suggestions for Agency Administrators* (Washington: American Bar Association 2002)(online at http://www.abanet.org/child/rclji/cp_agency.pdf).

King, Michael, and Judith Trowell. *Children's Welfare and the Law: The Limits of Legal Intervention* (London: Sage 1992).

Laver, Mimi. *Foundations for Success: Strengthening Your Agency Attorney Office* (Washington: American Bar Association, C. Sandt and S. Small Inada eds. 1999).

National Council of Juvenile and Family Court Judges, *Adoption and Permanency Guidelines: Improving Court Practice in Child Abuse and Neglect Cases* (Reno, Nevada: 2000).

National Council of Juvenile and Family Court Judges, *Court, Agency and Community Collaboration* (Reno, Nevada: 2000).

National Council of Juvenile and Family Court Judges, *Resource Guidelines: Improving Court Practice in Child Abuse and Neglect Cases* (Reno, Nevada: 1995).

Rauber, Diane Boyd. *Court Improvement Progress Report 2004* (Washington: American Bar Association, M. Laver ed. 2004)(online at http://www.abanet.org/child/cipcatalog/home.html).

Segal, Ellen. *Evaluating and Improving Child Welfare Legal Representation: Self-Assessment and Commentary* (Chicago: American Bar Association 1985).

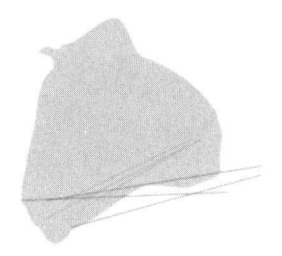

Index

A

Access to court 81
Adoption and Safe Families Act ... 9
 ASFA .. 9, 10, 29, 49, 50, 51, 52, 53, 55, 56, 57, 59, 60, 61, 63, 66, 68, 73, 91
Adoption Assistance and Child Welfare Act 9
Agency attorneys 52, 103, 145
 Correcting agency practices....... 87
 Delays....................................... 108
 Educating agency attorneys   23, 93
 Inadequate preparation 106
 Practice standards 137
 Protecting caseworkers 112
 Reference materials for agency attorneys 28
 Services agency attorneys should provide 135
 What agency attorneys should do 36
Agency-court project
 Purpose 20
 Successful projects 21
Agency-court relations 38, 94
Appeals 40, 41, 46, 88, 90, 91, 113, 126

 Attorneys refuse to pursue 42, 142
 Legal basis.................................. 45
 Planning 41, 43
 Preparing to file 114
Appearance in court 99, 101, 103, 108, 122

C

Caseflow management 124
Casework from the bench 86, 88
Child witness reform 84, 85
Complaints about judges
 By agencies 86
 Court calendar 128
 Judge bashing 110
 Judges who "shoot from the hip" 112
 Judges who do not appreciate the need for permanency 115
 Judges who refuse to make required findings 50
 Judges who refuse to remove endangered children or terminate parental rights 113
 Judicial disinterest 51
 Judicial misconduct 117, 118

159

Succumbing to worker
  complaints............................ 118
Complaints by judges
  Agency case preparation 102
  Agency court reports................ 104
  Agency testimony 105
  Casework................................... 101
  Frequent requests for
    continuances 108
  Implementing judicial orders .. 101
  Parents are not present at
    hearings 108
  Pet peeves 100
  Poor preparation of expert
    witnesses 107
  Quality of case plans 101
  The wrong agency employees
    at hearings 103
**Complying with federal
requirements 51, 52, 54, 57,
58, 59, 73, 74**
Court appearances 101, 108
  Burden 103
  Children 122
  Problems 103
  Punctuality 99
  Videotaping 84
**Court delays 34, 35, 82,
108, 114, 122, 123**
**Court reports 15, 19, 61, 63, 70,
104, 105**

D

Delays .. 75, 82, 83, 91, 92, 94, 108
**Delinquents and status
offenders 50, 72, 74**

E
Expert witnesses
  Preparing to testify 80, 81, 107
  Waiting time 79

F
Federal reimbursement
  Eligibility..................................... 70

G
**General strategies for working
with courts 13**
  Key court staff............................ 18
  Meetings with the judge 13

J
Joint training .... See training
Judges
  Clarifying legal issues 17
  Court forms................................ 57
  Dealing with judges 17
  Federal reimbursement for
    training 30
  Interpreting ASFA...................... 53
  Meeting with judges 13
  Not implementing federal
    requirements 51
  Persuading judges to make
    judicial determinations........... 59
  Reference materials for judges... 28
  Role in interdisciplinary
    committees 17
  Sharing information.................... 33
  Special meetings 17
  Training judges 23, 26, 31
  Working with judges on
    legislative issues..................... 33

Judicial and bar education 25, 29, 30, 115

Judicial determinations...............59

Judicial disinterest 51

Judicial interference.............86, 87

Judicial misconduct 117, 118

Juvenile court problems............127

Juvenile court reform 35, 84, 122, 123, 124, 128

Juvenile courts..... 46, 52, 58, 126, 148

    Caseload standards................... 128

    Cooperation regarding legislation 33

    Improving juvenile courts......... 124

    Requests for resources................ 34

    Staffing 18

    Systematically improving juvenile courts........................ 35

    Understanding juvenile courts... 97

    What child welfare administrators should know. 124

L

Legislation 33, 56, 88

M

Meetings

    Agency-court meetings 16, 19, 25, 30, 40, 80, 88, 107

    Meetings with agency staff 18

    Meetings with the judge 13, 14, 15, 16, 17, 18, 19, 38, 52, 111, 116

O

Organization and operations of juvenile courts 124

P

Paralegals or other specialized staff 38, 39, 40, 103, 141, 144

Permanency 50, 55, 115

    Permanency hearings 68, 69, 70

    Permanency plan 61, 62

    Permanency plans..... 100, 121, 128

R

Reasonable efforts.... 9, 25, 52, 55, 56, 60, 61, 62, 63, 64, 65, 73

Reports 15, 16, 109, 136

    Complaints about reports..... 104, 112

    Purpose of reports 105

    What judges want 98

Reviews 67

    Six-month reviews.................66, 67

    Voluntary placements 70

Reviews of voluntary placements................................. 70

S

Success in court 10, 89, 92, 130, 148

    Agency-court collaboration 94

    Agency-court cooperation 21, 70

    Appeals.............. 40, 41, 43, 46, 113

    Meetings 13

    Training................................23, 31

T

Termination of parental rights....... 39, 40, 45, 46, 63, 65, 68, 91, 92, 103, 125, 145

Testimony 66, 80, 81, 84, 94, 98, 99, 100, 103, 107, 110

    Agency testimony.............. 105, 106

Judicial testimony....................... 34
Preparation................................ 56

Training 23, 24, 25, 26, 28, 29, 133, 134, 138, 139, 144

V

Voluntary placements 70

W

Waiting time ... 75, 77, 78, 82, 103, 108
Caseworker 35, 74
Expert witnesses 79

Notes

Notes